D0645869

HOW TO USE THE POWER OF COLOR, AFFIRMATIONS, AND CREATIVE VISUALIZATIONS TO TRANSFORM YOUR LIFE

A FIRESIDE BOOK
PUBLISHED BY SIMON & SCHUSTER INC.
NEW YORK LONDON TORONTO SYDNEY TOKYO SINGAPORE

□ □ □

COLOR SYNERGY

PATRICIA GEORGE
DINAH LOVETT

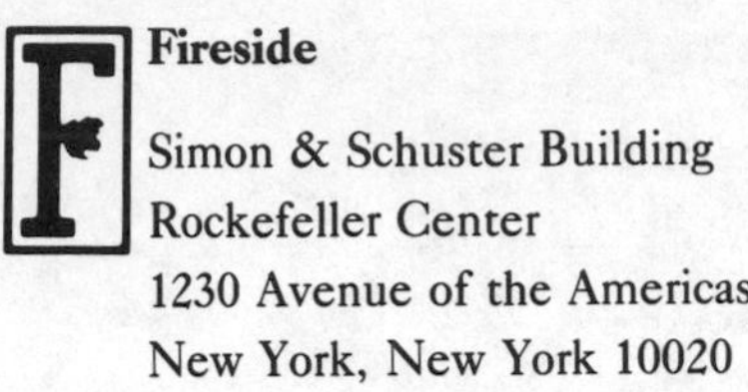

Fireside
Simon & Schuster Building
Rockefeller Center
1230 Avenue of the Americas
New York, New York 10020

DESIGNED BY DIANE STEVENSON/SNAP-HAUS GRAPHICS
Manufactured in the United States of America

10 9 8 7 6 5 4 3 2 1

Library of Congress Cataloging in Publication Data
George, Patricia.
Color synergy / Patricia George, Dinah Lovett.
p. cm.
1. Color—Psychological aspects. 2. Self-actualization
(Psychology) 3. Conduct of life. 4. Symbolism of colors.
I. Lovett, Dinah. II. Title.
BF789.C7G46 1990
158'.1—dc20 90-30734
CIP

ISBN 0-671-68409-4

To Dickie, Brian, and our families and friends.

Where we love, we live.

□ □ □

ACKNOWLEDGMENTS

We wish to thank Helen Leflar, Christy Dickey, Merle Lovett, and Laura Woodroof.

□ □ □

FOREWORD

Throughout this book we have referred to the Supreme Being as Father or God. We've used these terms because they are comfortable to us. If you wish to substitute your own special name, please do so. We've also used the pronoun "he" for convenience' sake.

□ □ □

CONTENTS

C H A P T E R I

CURING THE WITHOUT SYNDROME

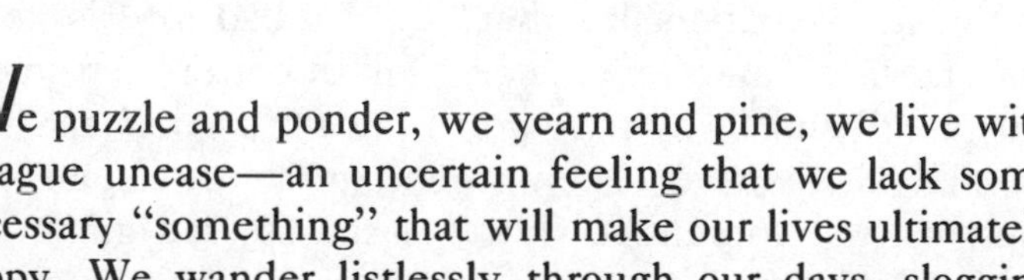

We puzzle and ponder, we yearn and pine, we live with a vague unease—an uncertain feeling that we lack some necessary "something" that will make our lives ultimately happy. We wander listlessly through our days, slogging through the quicksand of endless hours, wallowing in the slough of despond. Events move like molasses and self-pity stays with us like gum on our shoes.

We are mired in the dimension of the "not-yet," the "if-only," and the "I-had-no-choice." How very familiar is the old refrain, "but I can't help it"; we sing or listen to this nasal tune over and over.

These symptoms reveal a mysterious disease, one that is difficult to describe: it is an unfulfilled yearning, a vague sense that as individuals we are not complete, not "together."

This disease makes us wishy-washy, uncomfortable

with our bodies and our personalities, anxious, and unhappy. It colors careers, family relationships, physical health, love relationships, and it seeps into that intimate personal place within us where our spiritual being resides.

This disease prevents us from achieving that clean, exultant joy that comes from knowing we are functional, contributing, adult, compassionate, and wise. It prevents us from being complete human beings, the beings God created to inhabit this beautiful world. This manifestation of spiritual-emotional-psychological disquiet is called the "Without Syndrome."

We are without confidence, without love, without hope, without purpose, without courage, and without character. And we are without the means to obtain these attributes.

In the battle for happiness, apathy and passivity are the enemies. When life is governed by fears, happiness cannot be attained because we are afraid to start—afraid to try for it. We rationalize that "even a bad love is better than no love" and "even a bad job is better than unemployment" and "why try when I know I'll fail?" and "it's too difficult." So we wallow around in the status quo, content, yet not content, to live out the blessed gift of life wrapped in cotton fleece, too frightened to take a chance or risk losing the familiar, comfortable drudgery we've chosen. Life stretches out in front of us like an endless putty-colored ribbon.

Picture this type of life as it might be mapped on a heart monitor screen: a dead person's line is flat—no blips, no ups, and no downs. A living person's heart line bounces all over the screen, and while the beat pattern is steady, the line is interesting, moving, and *alive!*

Take a moment to consider your life. Is it dull and murky, slow and sodden? Do you feel trapped and unloved? Are you a victim? Is fear the measure by which you plan your activities? Do you see life as something to be endured, something to "get through"?

Some people never let go of old pain and old guilt. They hold their hurts close to them and tend them lovingly. Some people are cynical and distrusting, for hasn't life dealt them a hand and isn't it their lot to play the hand out according to a self-imposed fatalistic program?

Those who always look to be wronged, or anticipate being disappointed or betrayed, shut out life in its entirety. Some people spend all the energy they can muster protecting themselves from pain, and they will not hope because hope makes them vulnerable. Lack of hope distances human beings from what human beings want, and those people believe that hope will somehow doom them to loss. To live with hope, they say, is stupid because it sets one up for rejection and failure—they detach themselves from life and say, "Not again—not me—I've been hurt before."

Poet Robert Frost tells us that something in the cosmos doesn't love a wall, and he's right. If we expend precious energy in erecting walls that protect us, we shut out limitless possibilities for happiness. The person who denies the right and responsibility for his personal happiness denies himself the glory of hope, and dooms himself to a life of dread and disillusion. In the end, he does more damage to himself than could be done to him by others.

Merle Stein, author of *Hearts That We Broke Long Ago*, believes that "A heart frozen against pain also stifles joy." Hope is the incentive which powers us along the life journey. Ms. Stein says that "Hope is a way of healing, the stroke of grace that transcends all the pain, a kind of light of the soul without which our hearts could never feast or we become the selves we were meant to be." Life is not a crapshoot.

If you do not see yourself in the preceding paragraphs,

yet your life is full of sorrow and pain and lack, you may be dealing with another forbidding aspect of life. If your life is not presently full and exciting, filled with what appears to be too much to do, too much to think about, too much to achieve, and too much to learn, and if you are not open and responsive to life stimulants, you may be wrestling with the dreaded . . .

□ *THWART MONSTER* □

As long as we are whining about life, let's ask ourselves another series of questions. Why, when we finally begin to move forward and show signs of emotional growth, are our plans immediately scotched and our newfound courage dried up? Why, when we finally grasp something or some idea that appears real and solid, or when we get a foothold on the slippery road to success, do our feet slip and our grips loosen?

Surely, we whimper, our failure is not our fault! Surely we've done everything right. Something always halts us in every endeavor; some mysterious force stops us cold. Someone else gets the job, someone else finds the perfect mate, someone else knocks a home run in the financial game. How mean-spirited and small, we observe, not to be happy for someone else's good fortune. But, in the back of our minds, aren't we a teeny bit jealous, a mite disgruntled with someone else's success?

The track of the Thwart Monster is plain. His footprints seem to glow in the dark night of our lives, and his evil cackle booms menacingly from the dark void. When we fall on our faces, the Thwart Monster rejoices! He comes out of nowhere to punish us—for are we not his innocent victims? We are weak, we pout, and we have no weapons to fight him.

Some victims blame others for their failures. Some martyrs wallow in their pain. Some vain people turn inward and try to justify themselves by feeling persecuted. Some cowards simply refuse to know what they know: that their lives are their responsibilities and their happiness is a conscious choice. They refuse to know that human beings are endowed with a force stronger than any tangible or intangible earthly power, and that they possess vast resources which lie dormant within them.

A woman once stated that she was always third or fifth or tenth in the pecking order of life. And that she knew people who were "first." She identified these chosen ones because they projected some inner shine, some added dimension, and the "first" ones strutted about like peacocks, secure in the knowledge that they mattered. She envied these paragons because she was always third. Or fifth. Or tenth. She figured it was just the luck of the draw, and therefore contented herself with a rampant case of the Without Syndrome and let the Thwart Monster pound her into mush. Drab gray was the color of her life, and her closed heart barely beat. She did, however, believe that she should be commended for her bravery and endurance. Paul Simon sang this woman's life: a good day had no rain, and a bad day was when she lay in bed and thought of things that might have been.

When dearest wishes lie withered in a cold breast and dreams ignite, then flicker away, the Thwart Monster has found another victim. Depression strikes and anger grows and consumes. A pity-party gets thrown and the only guest is the host.

How can we hope when blackness seeps into the very depths of our hearts? How can we pick ourselves up one more time and try again? How can we go out every day and get our noses bloodied, only to rise and do the same again the next day?

This book is about hope, and hope is the greatest tonic

in life, for without it we die unborn. This is a practical handbook on how to hope, succeed, love and be loved, prosper and live fully. The process requires no special equipment or clothing, no special diet or training. This process begins immediately—or whenever you decide to face the enemies. You may work at your own pace and the course costs no money.

It does, however, require a payment more valuable than money. To cure the Without Syndrome and defeat the Thwart Monster, you must prepare yourself to be brutally honest, courageous, and brave, dedicated to truth and action, ready to receive abundance, and able to follow simple instructions.

The object of the game is to find the cure for the Without Syndrome, and in so doing, to banish the Thwart Monster. The object of the game is to become a whole, functional, healthy, spiritual human being.

Wait just a minute! What is a "spiritual" human being? Must I learn to project astrally? Is this some voodoo, psychic mumbo jumbo?

Don't get hysterical. Read on.

□ *TEN CHARACTERISTICS OF A SPIRITUAL PERSON* □

A "spiritual" person possesses, among other traits, the following characteristics. He is:

□ INSIGHTFUL. A person who is attuned spiritually works toward understanding himself and others. He studies the human condition, even unto pain and cruelty, in order to obtain knowledge and information. Having insight is not a product of genes or chromosomes; it is the result of conscientious observation. The spiritual one simply notices things and remembers what he notices. He files this information away for future reference and comparison. His head is in the game. He observes.

□ RESOURCEFUL. There's more than one way to solve problems, more than one place to obtain information, more than one avenue to explore. For any quandary, there are many internal and external resources to tap. There is no such thing as an immovable object, speaking generally. There are always several viable answers to life's questions. If a person gives up the first time he meets with resistance, he is not a victim, he is a quitter. The spiritual person constantly searches for ways in which to deal with circumstances. The spiritual person thinks.

□ DISCERNING. We are all endowed with a certain amount of native intelligence, and we can use this to spot false or dishonest ploys. Utilize a basic thought process to assimilate information and separate the true from the untrue. Know that the unreal is nothing and can have no value, but the genuine is to be honored and revered. You do not have to be an Einstein to make value judgments. Beware of fakes, charlatans, snake-oil salesmen, the corrupt, the contemptible, and the criminal. The spiritual person discriminates.

□ INTUITIVE. Intuition is the sixth sense, the hunch, that sneaky feeling. Into the turmoil of our busy minds, the Father whispers to us constantly. It is with our intuition that we subconsciously hear these messages. Trust your instincts. Do you remember when your teacher admonished you to go with your first inclination in answering test questions? Usually, if you messed with an answer until your mind was completely muddled, you missed the answer entirely. So, go with your gut reaction and never go against your better judgment. The spiritual person listens.

□ AWAKENING. If we are continually aware of changing conditions, of areas of knowledge available to us, of spontaneous opportunities, we awaken. We rouse the slumbering soul inside us and we absorb new ideas like sponges. How exciting life is, how magnificent in its intricacy! Anticipate the next hour—day—month—and the future! What a heady feeling to know that we have freedom and movement, that we can adapt and change to fit each new sunrise. The spiritual person is *ready;* he tingles, he expands.

□ IDEALISTIC. Hold truth inviolate. A code of morality is a code of ideals, something necessary to all spiritual beings for survival. Upon our ideals will we stand or fall. Embrace reality, shun hypocrisy. Run from ignorance, rise above slothfulness. Be true, steadfast, honorable. Recognize the superiority of no man's mind above your own for making your decisions. Formulate strong, positive standards to live by and cling to them. Your high standards will bring you through any crisis and will help you make good decisions, the correct decisions for you. The spiritual person believes.

□ PRINCIPLED. Closely associated with ideals are principles; principles are ideals in action. There must be some activities in which we do not participate. There are others in which we are always involved. A spiritual person does not compromise his principles. He lives up to his ideals in every act or thought. He is strong in his idea of what is right, just, and honorable, and although it is good to hear all viewpoints, the spiritual person knows what he knows and acts upon it. He stands his ground.

□ FEELING. An emotion is a feeling which begins in the mind and colors reactions. It is an instinctive response to life's myriad situations. Your personal code of ethics determines your response, and this response is a "feeling." Strong or weak, we all experience emotions at every moment of the day. Anger, happiness, and peace are emotions. Feelings give life depth and texture. Feelings send us soaring in delight or languishing in despair. Sometimes we get chill bumps; this is a physical sign of an emotion or feeling. The spiritual person responds.

□ POSITIVE. Moving forward and upward, facing the Light, the spiritual human being repels negativity, eschews apathy, and shuns destructive thoughts, words, and deeds. He does not think a negative thought unless he immediately cancels it out with a positive one. The pessimist, in the end, may be proved right, but the optimist has a better time on the trip. Positivity creates positivity—it is magnetic. The positive person draws unto himself positive situations and feelings. The negative person will soon have no friends, for no one likes to hear awfulness all the time. The spiritual person looks for good; he is confident.

□ POWERFUL. Who can resist the power of the human mind coupled with the power of the Father? No force is stronger, no army mightier, no obstacle immovable when the human mind and the Father unite. The spiritual person depends upon and knows his power, and wields it with justice, kindness, and positive ambition. The spiritual person is strong and capable, a person of ability.

It is positively within the realm of the doable when you decide to be a spiritual being. All you must do is make up your mind. Go back to basics: recognize that you may *choose* to be honest and brave. Align yourself with the Father and let Him guide you to success and happiness. He wants us to be happy, but it is in our power to be miserable just as it is in our power to be happy.

Mankind has a desperate need, especially today, for heroes. We need role models, human beings who depict the heroic possibilities of man's nature. From an informal opinion poll of predominantly middle-class clerical workers, startling information was gained about who we consider as heroes or heroic:

GEORGE WASHINGTON	BILL COSBY
DOROTHY PARKER	ROGER STAUBACH
BARBARA WALTERS	ROSEANNE BARR
JOHN F. KENNEDY	JOAN OF ARC
GERALDINE FERRARO	MARILYN MONROE
MARTIN LUTHER KING, JR.	FLORENCE GRIFFITH-JOYNER

When the same persons were asked to list what traits or characteristics in others are most admired, they named the following (in order of most admired first):

HONESTY
SENSE OF HUMOR
INDIVIDUALISM

These four attributes tied for fourth: compassion, friendliness, intelligence, and confidence.

Respondents were vehement in their answers to "What traits do you most despise?"

TELLING LIES (DISHONESTY)
CONCEIT
HYPOCRISY
SELF-PITY
FALSENESS

Many of those polled wrote lengthy paragraphs about their admiration of those who could stand up for what they believe, those who were true to themselves, and those who displayed confidence, sensitivity, and honorable behavior. It is within each of us to exhibit these heroic traits and to demonstrate them every day.

For our children's sake, for the sake of people all over

the earth, for our friends, neighbors, and family, determine to rise to the heroic possibilities within you. Give us heroes!

□ *PLAN OF ACTION* □

If you are sick to death of the Without Syndrome and your daily bout with the Thwart Monster, you may want to investigate how to become a spiritual person. Through this investigation, you will discover that special person who lives in your body. Work through these few instructions.

□ ROUSE THE INNER SELF. When a situation hits you where you live, recognize the place inside you where this feeling begins. Start from there. Under the subterfuge—the persona you wear around others—lives a delicate being. Gently probe your inner self and, while protecting its soft underbelly, awaken that being and alert it to new stimuli. Have a conversation with yourself. This is where you must be brutally honest. If you are a whiner, admit it. You do not have to continue to be a whiner, but the first must in becoming a heroic person is to identify the traits that prevent you from being happy and successful. If you harbor hatred for another, consciously look at it, even though seeing that characteristic is most uncomfortable. If you are basically lazy and have no ambition, so be it. But find out those things about yourself and be aware of them. You must know who your enemy is before you challenge it to do battle. Tread carefully but diligently here; you are dealing with the real you.

□ REACH FOR KNOWLEDGE. Strive to attain that plateau where clear sight identifies "real" as authentic and "unreal" as valueless. This might hurt a little: just because you earnestly want to be a compassionate person, wanting it does not make you one; and just because you want to be thought of as wise does not give you wisdom. Now is the time to get down and dirty with the real you. This identification process takes place in your rational mind. When reason rules your thoughts and behavior, the margin for error slims to a razor's edge. Always ask yourself what is reasonable, what is rational, what is true, what is correct based on the knowledge you possess. Constantly gather knowledge and store it away. The gathering of knowledge applies to self-exploration as well as to external exploration.

Expand on your journey through the self by learning new skills and experimenting. Expand your interests and open up; you will automatically enhance the quality of your life. Don't be content to recycle the information you already possess. Find out, search out, and consider (with no limitations) what it might be like to know something new.

A woman once lived a stagnant existence, but she explored her inner self and determined to remedy her stagnation. She decided to learn some new skills, and she decided to take action in a few areas in which her interest was piqued. She learned a smattering of the language of the deaf—signing. She took herself to a planetarium and gazed at the starred and planeted ceiling. She examined the motor of her automobile and identified the engine, radiator, air filter, battery, and cables.

All these activities cost her no money and required very little effort. The benefits were astounding, for the woman gained depth, compassion, appreciation, and confidence.

Consider these words and topics and see what pops into your own mind. Would you be interested in checking out some of these areas?

Library, zoo, plant nursery, gardening, volunteer work at hospitals, photography, upholstery, museums, stock market, musical instruments, acting, ceramics, dancing, oceanography, speech-writing, quilting, computers, antiques, retail marketing, education.

The areas are vast and the possibilities limitless.

Grow through expanding the limits of your mind, grow through searching, filtering, discarding, and retaining new information.

□ PRACTICE SELF-DISCIPLINE while you train your mind. You can teach your mind to think. Follow a rational process of thinking and base every learning attempt on the same ideals: reason and purpose. Base every learning attempt on spiritual values: truth and love. You can shape your mind and heart to work together, to focus sharply on ideas and circumstances. When the mind and the heart (the center of emotion) work together, beauty and knowledge are one, emotion and intellect function smoothly. There is no higher sense of achievement.

A popular belief today, and a valid one, is the idea that human beings play "old tapes" in the mind. We condition ourselves to react in certain ways. It is a habit. When you observe your lover flirting, you immediately engage the "jealous" tape. When someone disagrees with you, the "I-want-my-way" tape begins. When you experience some disappointment, the "woe-is-me" tape clicks into action. Be aware that you play old tapes in your mind; identify the tapes and recognize that you can change them. This is self-discipline of the mind.

□ LIVE! Good things naturally come to those who love their lives, to those who savor every moment. Your feet and mind are not set in cement. Take action! Formulate a constructive reasoning process and make it into a new tape. Employ your native intelligence and excel; go beyond what you know today and gather knowledge to use tomorrow. Embark on an opportunity-spotting reorientation of the mind.

Don't let a moment of this precious life get by you. Spend those moments to grow and learn. Let the mind and the heart soar together. Know total joy when your reasoning mind and loving heart join forces as you face a rational universe. New cycles of life await you! Practice being happy and excited about living your life.

And most important: Fight. Human beings possess enormous power, incredible tenacity, overwhelming energy. Use this storehouse of might to wage a heroic battle—the battle for your purposeful, happy existence.

Fight against shame, self-pity, guilt, dishonor, despair, cruelty, apathy, stupidity, and cowardice.

Fight for honor, virtue, pride, spiritual growth, truth, beauty, light, hope, heroism, love, productivity, and the achievement of goals.

Don't let anyone stop you and don't let your fears govern your life. Take risks. Get rid of old tapes and prepare some new ones. Don't let the fire of ardent life-living go out, spark by irreplaceable spark, by wading through a swamp of turbulent discord in your mind. Take charge of yourself and don't just exist—fervently live your life! Be bold!

C H A P T E R II

MOTIVATION AND GOAL-SETTING

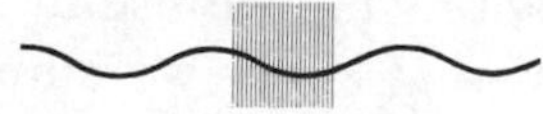

"If you have built castles in the air, your work need not be lost; that is where they should be. Now put the foundations under them." Henry David Thoreau eloquently introduces this chapter on motivation and goal-setting, for now we intend to put foundations under our castles in the air.

Here we are, pumped with adrenaline, but where do we go with all this energy? Ancient wise ones say that a long journey begins with a single step. But first we must know where we are going and what goal we will accomplish when we get there.

It follows as the night unto the day that people who set and accomplish goals are happier than those who drift through their lives without purpose, rudderless. The setting and achieving of personal goals are linked directly to self-esteem, how we feel about ourselves.

The concept of self-esteem has been worked to death, and rightfully so, because happiness is only possible to one who holds himself in high regard—one who believes himself worthy of happiness, and that happiness is his human birthright. A mountain of information is available explaining just exactly what self-esteem is, how to have good self-esteem, and how to conquer poor self-esteem. Paul Simon's "One Trick Pony" dances, prances, glances, and glides. The pony knows only one trick, but he performs it with pride. Many of us have only "one trick," but if we perform it creatively, passionately, and with every ounce of our potential, then one trick is all we need.

Self-esteem is the judgment we pass on ourselves. "Ego" and "I" describe self-esteem. It is depicted not in our thoughts, but with what we use to think; it is not our decisions, but with what entity we employ to make those decisions; it is not our emotions, but what we feel emotions with. We make decisions based on what we think is appropriate for us; how we feel about ourselves determines what is appropriate. If you believe that you are worthy of happiness, then you have given yourself permission to seek happiness and attain it. If you believe that basically you are no good, have no talent or very little, have been "bad," and don't deserve to be happy, then you will search unrelentingly for what makes you miserable. Arnold Bennett writes, "If egotism means a terrific interest in one's self, egotism is absolutely essential to efficient living."

Every aspect of our being is affected, one way or another, by the way we evaluate ourselves. What we desire and dream for is directly connected with what we believe we deserve. How we act and react, what we stand for, our principles and ideals, all spring directly from the rep we've acquired with ourselves.

Before you can be a successful, happy person, first you must *be*. Your own self-esteem leads you to this judgment. In order to survive, you must be true to your sovereign, rational self. If this appears to be supremely egotistical, so be it. No one can be you as efficiently as you can; no one can assimilate, identify, and analyze yourself as truly as you can. No one else is qualified to make decisions for you but you. The person you choose to be is the actualization of your self-esteem. If you let others determine what is best for you, if you let them tell you who you are, then you are doomed to unhappiness. Your self-esteem must be healthy and competent and active. What you choose as your goals, and the path you take to further the achievement of them, is steered by your basic sense of self-worth.

Some people are driven: they thrust themselves aggressively into their lives, spurred onward by the basic, almost frantic need to achieve goals. Others never seem to find a goal, even a small one, to work toward. In this area, as in all others, successful, happy people must be guided by reason and full-blown, healthy self-esteem.

A study of goal-setting reveals many facets of the topic: how to do it, how many, what, when, why, and so on. Contemplate yourself and your personal situation. Assume that you wish to achieve a goal and thereby bolster your self-esteem.

Sink down into that intimate personal place where you carefully guard your being—who you really are and what you believe. Be honest now. If your all-consuming passion at this moment is to get your mother off your back, or if you are driven by the need to accumulate wealth, or if your matchbook collection is all that keeps you interested and moves you forward, okay. Just acknowledge it and go on. (This is facetious, but occasionally we *are* motivated by "bad things" like revenge, pity, anger, and by elementary needs, like the need for admiration or the desire for a moment's silence.) If that is the case, fine. It's okay to be motivated by these things at times. Noel Coward said, "Your motivation is your pay packet on Friday. Now get on with it." What we are looking for is not a religious crusade; we simply want to know about reasonable goal-setting and motivation.

The authors conducted an informal poll among their

fellows, asking them to write a short note about goal-setting and what motivates them to achieve goals, or even set them. Disregarding the high-toned, noble paragraphs we all write because we want others to think us grand, there appeared some interesting information.

One young single mother, Laura, was initially frustrated when she first began to set goals, write them down, and later review them. It seemed she had to write down the same goals over and over. "To be a good mother" is, in fact, a worthy goal, but it is an ongoing thing, and if you write it on your list of goals, you never get to mark it off. "To be a good person" is dandy, but if you mark off that one, you'll probably be sprouting wings and carrying a harp. "World peace" is somewhat grandiose; "to open the mail" is a little shortsighted, and "to look better than Belinda" is downright tacky.

However, Laura did zero in on some great goals. She wanted to change her present course of griping-fussing-irritation after a hard day's work and to present a mentally healthy, happy image to her children instead. Laura wanted her children to be whole, healthy, and confident, with space and freedom to be themselves and to make their own good decisions. She set out to demonstrate a role model encompassing these traits, and to teach her children a workable method for making good decisions. This is a swell goal, and one which is accomplishable and promises wonderful rewards. This young woman wanted to give her children wings to fly and a good foundation from which to take off. Bravo!

How is she doing it? Well, the first step she took was to study intensely her own behavior, her own ideals and principles and her own emotions. Then Laura began to gather information. She read books and spoke with knowledgeable others, her friends, and family. She found that she took her office woes home with her—big mistake. She found that she could, if she chose, let irritation slide off her back like rain off a swan. She discovered that any little snippets of irritation endured at the office could be banished by the loving acceptance and attention she received from her kids. Earthshaking, no, but miraculous? Yes. She was motivated by a strong desire to change the atmosphere in her home and her relationship with her children. Laura found the *personal power* to set and achieve her goals.

One of the authors tells a story of the very first time she consciously set a goal and achieved it. One day, as she contemplated the random shelving of books in her bookcase, she decided to write her name in every one, restack them, and clean up the whole shebang. This silly little goal became a holy quest, for she had hundreds of books, hardback and paperback, pamphlets and stapled-together papers. She sat on her hassock with a Bic medium-point blue pen and began to write her name in every book. The mailman came to the door—she scooped up the mail and laid it on the kitchen table for later. Chatty Lulu called, but it was "Later, Lulu, I'm busy now." She sat there for several hours, but she wrote her name in every book, stacked it neatly, according to size, in the bookcase, and dusted the whole area. Big deal, you observe. And so it is.

In achieving that simple goal, the author discovered the joy of setting a goal and being motivated to complete it. If goal-setting sparked such a wondrous sense of satisfaction from such a tiny task, could it work for higher, more difficult applications? You bet.

The other author states frankly that she is motivated by her partner. She says, "*You* motivate me to start" researching, "but somewhere along the line, I become motivated all by myself, and the motivation becomes mine, the goal is mine, and the accomplishment belongs to me."

Let's say you work with a belligerent woman whose forked tongue deals you misery, but her work product is top-of-the-line. You've thrashed around with this problem until the world looked level, and had your feelings hurt, been stomp-footed angry, and unendurably frustrated. So, after you throw your series of tantrums, you begin to deal constructively with the problem. Ask yourself: What do I want to happen? Well, ideally, you'd like the woman to move to Mars, but then her beautiful work would be denied you. Also ideally, *you'd* like to move to Mars to get away from her acid tongue, but the result is the same. Somewhere in the middle is probably the right answer: maybe you just want her to shut up and do her job.

We all run into people we simply cannot stand, and vice versa. Problems in the workplace are as varied as there are people who work. We never know the problems, bitterness, and loves of any other human being—we barely know ourselves that well. Many possibilities exist which might make Ms. Acid-Tongue speak so repugnantly, but it is not our problem. Again: her problems do not belong to us. We are not in charge of her. We are only in charge of ourselves and how we will react or not react to any situation. She is obviously suffering from either the Without Syndrome or the Thwart Monster, or a nasty combination of both.

Now that the monkey is off your back, a number of choices reveal themselves. You can fret about it and gnash your teeth or you can even rend your garments, but you spend a huge amount of energy in these activities and receive nothing for them in return but a headache and an upset stomach. What your coworker does and says diminishes you not in the slightest degree. You can put a stop to outrage by saying no. Say the word no in your mind and remove yourself from participating in her drama. Do not respond to anything but courteous appeals. Say nothing when a tirade of unfair accusations is heaped upon you. Simply do not respond. You can do that, you know.

Or, if you just can't keep your hands off, you might try reasoning with her—the old come-let-us-reason-together plan. But do not expect her to see the light and say, "Thank you, thank you, you've changed my life!" That response is simply not reasonable.

What *is* reasonable is your goal: to get along and not allow outside influences to ruin your pleasant day and your positive attitude.

The preceding paragraphs denote small goals, but human beings do not exist by striving for one all-encompassing passionate aim. Fulfilling life is the setting and completing of a number of small goals, several larger goals, and a few holy quests.

To learn elementary goal-setting and motivation, seek out a tiny goal, one that can be achieved in a matter of minutes. Then do it. Just do it.

Congratulations. Now you know the basic fundamental law of goal-setting and motivation: just do it.

Let's go on to some woolly-boogers, some goals which require time, attention to detail, long-term commitment, and a quantity of intense energy. These we'll call "life" goals.

The most difficult phase of goal-setting and finding the motivation to achieve life goals (those aims which transcend the ordinary, like "What do you want to be when you grow up?") is to answer, honestly, the question: What do you want?

□ *WHAT DO YOU WANT?* □

Sometimes the answer to that question is "pie" or "all the money in the world" or "Tom Cruise." We sidestep the responsibility for answering that question by being funny or vague, and occasionally we become deaf and change the subject. Why? Because it is such an excruciatingly difficult question to answer. Stating what you want, even to yourself, simply bowls you over! We kinda know what we want or how we'll feel when we get it, but getting to the real answer of "What do you want?" is like giving birth.

In stating exactly what we want, we imply that we are ready to commit to getting it. This is not so. Sometimes seven million dollars in small bills is a fervent wish, but if you got them, you wouldn't want the tax problem that travels close behind.

Fantasies are not goals, and though we may really, really want our fantasies to come true, they are not reasonable and rational. Fantasies, we believe, must be a part of any happy person's being. We find out so much from fantasies, and they are so emotionally and mentally healthy in their place. On a graph, however, gritty reality perches on one end and fantasies fall off the other. Dreams, now, and desires/wishes/hopes lie right in the middle of the graph. These are attainable, worthy, delightful considerations. And, terrifically, you *can* make your dreams come true!

For material objects, "What do you want?" is the only way to focus your desire. The correct question when considering a situation or a circumstance, however, is to ask, "What do you want to happen?" How do you envision the situation resolving itself? What position will you be in when the dust settles?

□ *WHAT DO YOU WANT TO BE WHEN YOU GROW UP?* □

You do not have to know what you want to be when you grow up by a certain age. There is no deadline for deciding about your career. You can even change your entire career in the middle of the stream. Nowhere is it written that by the time you graduate from college, you *must* know what you want to be. So take the pressure off and think, within a casual atmosphere, about career/job/self-image, etc.

Find out what you really want to be by answering the following questions:

1. What makes me feel good? What activity, when I perform it, promotes a positive feeling of accomplishment, pride, self-esteem, strength, fun, and enjoyment inside me? What activity makes me feel warm inside? For what do I possess an intense desire?

2. Do I like to do it? Am I compelled to do it? Do I love the planning and carrying out of the tasks that bring me to achievement?

Consider being a secretary. Do I feel good when I type a document or take a phone message correctly? Am I excited when I greet clients or customers? Does the come-and-go of many people stimulate me? Does working closely with other people in a team effort give me satisfaction? Am I happy when I finish a day's work?

3. What compensation do I expect from my career? Am I satisfied with the opportunities available in this area? Is my salary acceptable? Do I receive my compensation from feedback from others? Am I satisfied when I reach thc point when my own mind tells me "good job"?

4. Do my career goals fit my circumstances? What accommodations am I willing to make in order to achieve my career goals? Are any accommodations necessary? What must I do first in order to pursue my chosen career goals?

5. Do I have the dedication required to achieve the goal, the stamina to stay with it? Can I do away with concepts in my personal life that are limiting? Will I enjoy the journey, the trip I take to achieve my goal?

□ *THE NEXT STEP* □

Now comes the easy part: figuring out how to achieve goals. All you need to do is make a plan. If you have discovered what you like to do, even by accident, then you have a pretty good idea what must be done in order to get where you want to be career-wise. If you wish to own a bakery, you already know that you must know how to bake. If you wish to be a brain surgeon, it's pretty clear that you must attend medical school. And don't be frightened by what you think may be your own shortcomings or lack of education or wherewithal. Professionals built the *Titanic*, amateurs built the ark.

Never settle for second best, unless that is exactly what you want. Sandy had a talent for designing jewelry. All her pieces looked professional and were beautifully done—she worked on her craft to her maximum potential. She did not stint on her creations. When she decided she wanted to sell her jewelry on the open market, she did not settle for hawking her wares on the street corner. Sandy borrowed a briefcase, stuck in a few samples, and took herself to the Dallas Apparel Mart. She started knocking on showroom doors. At the end of the day, she had found a showroom to handle her product. All she had to do was provide samples and her market representatives took the orders. Sandy filled the orders, shipped them, paid her reps their commissions, and pocketed a sweet profit.

Don't be afraid to play with the big boys. Try 'em on. Learn to take risks. Follow your plan.

□ *MAKING THE PLAN* □

Write down your plan. Write down your goal in as much detail as you can. Don't charge into the battle without knowing the plan. Stephen Leacock wrote, in his Nonsense Novels, that "Lord Ronald said nothing; he flung himself from the room, flung himself upon his horse and rode madly off in all directions." Don't be another Lord Ronald. Write it down.

While you are writing, see yourself in your mind achieving the goal. See yourself successfully moving through the days of your life fulfilled, excited, motivated, achieving. See scenes in which you perform your chosen work brilliantly. See what you are wearing, see your surroundings, feel what it means to stand atop the highest peak of success in your career. See yourself standing alone and strong, facing an open universe with calm acceptance. Look into the distance and see the worlds you have conquered. Affirm your complete success.

Remember these pictures. Remember these feelings.

Write down each step of the way. Regarding the bakery:

1. You'll need a shop or a place in your home.
2. Do you have the necessary tools? Oven, spatula, cake pans, recipes, potholders?
3. Do you have the necessary skills? Will a class in cake-decorating be helpful?
4. What about advertising? Will word-of-mouth get you enough business, or do radio/TV/newspapers look attractive? Can you meet the production demand if your business really takes off?
5. Can you keep records correctly? Do you need knowledge in this area?
6. What do you say when your first customer calls? Should you make a list of pertinent questions? Do you ask about size, color, flavor, decorations, occasion, specialty requirements?
7. Where can you get flour and sugar in bulk quantities?
8. Do you need a sales tax permit?
9. Will Doris watch your kids if you get in a bind?

Now don't get entranced with only the writing-down part of goal-setting; that is, don't think you've reached nirvana when you can write down great notes. Remember the screenplay *The More the Merrier* by Richard Flournoy and Lewis R. Foster? "There are two kinds of people: those who don't do what they want to do, so they write down in a diary about what they haven't done, and those who haven't time to write about it because they're out doing it." Be complete and do the job correctly, but gather your energy for action. And don't miss any ridiculous little thing. Nobody but yourself is going to read your list, so write down even the silliest concerns or the simplest requirements, the most basic fears.

Fears?

□ *HANDLING FEAR* □

Fear is limiting. Fear is scary. Fear makes us want to hide somewhere safe and not make a move. Fear defeats risk-taking which defeats achievement and success before we begin. Fear is common to all ages and to all people. It is universal. The Peanuts comic strip is popular because it depicts beliefs many people profess privately: "I have a new philosophy. I'm only going to dread one day at a time." Charles Schulz knows about human beings.

Learning to handle fear could be the single most important skill in life. Don't be timid. Remember what Kin Hubbard stated: "It's going to be fun to watch and see how long the meek can keep the earth after they inherit it."

Fear sabotages clarity and efficiency and undermines healthy self-esteem. Fear is a weapon of the Thwart Monster. Whatever we fear, we give energy to. Often when we are frozen by fear, we do not move forward because we fear making the wrong decision, and we think that particular decision will forever deprive us of something important—that one wrong move will immediately catapult us into hell. This notion is pure nonsense.

If you make a mistake, so what? Say, "Oops, made a mistake here!" and begin again. Don't spend all your time anticipating an ambush. Most of the things human beings fear never, ever happen anyway. We've wasted that energy anticipating the unknown instead of getting by it. A person who takes his self-esteem and sense of personal worth from himself is whole and brave. Those who wait for others to validate them like a parking ticket, those who wait for others to comment upon a chosen course of action, take who they are not from themselves but from others. Be who you are; don't be someone others put together like a misfitting puzzle. Be contemptuous of those moral bigots; rain praise upon those who stand tall and make their own decisions and make their own mistakes, for those people own, absolutely, their successes.

It doesn't matter if people laugh at you. They are laughing because they are afraid too, and a nervous giggle or a loud guffaw from anyone else doesn't make any difference. Theodore Roosevelt respected the man who fought in the arena, not those who sat in the grandstands and laughed. The man who faces his fears is truly noble; jeering spectators are garden-variety slugs.

Cut out your tongue if you ever hear yourself wail, "But what will other people *think*?" *You* be the one who aggressively takes action to face fear. *You* be the person who looks his fears in the eye and spits. *You* be the one who bravely faces the unknown and conquers evil. *You* try something new; *you* pick yourself up, dust off your bottom, and try again. And never mind the general public's opinion.

Sometimes fear can be a healthy emotion. It can be an instinctive safety warning which sounds an alert to danger. When the Klaxon horn of fear goes off in your head, immediately open up—look around—what is it that is fearful? An immediate response is not a fearful reaction; it is an aggressive action, the constructive reaction to fear. Make it a conscious practice to notice what causes the alarm to ring. It's no sin to be afraid, so let it come. But notice and learn from the things you feel afraid of.

You can tell a lot about a person if you know what he fears, and by the same token, you can learn much about yourself when you identify what you fear. Allow this information to sharpen your inner vision. When you come up against a fearful thing, externally or internally, don't immediately hunt a place to hide. Walk right up to it. Look for methods to handle the situation constructively. Avoid the intricate manufacture of an unreal answer; cease looking for a scapegoat. Don't waste energy trying to plea-bargain with the Father.

Fear *can* be handled, and the energy we use to run from the Thwart Monster can be used instead for positive purposes. We all experience fear at some point in life, but it does not have to shut us down. Consciously let panic open up the mind. Turn that burst of adrenaline to solving the problem, handling the frightening circumstance, overcoming the possibility of failure. To deal with fear effectively, simply pull the plug on its power; it will die on the spot.

The saddest situation is the one in which the players of life's drama/comedy are governed by their fears. Mark Twain said, "Courage is resistance to fear, mastery of fear—not absence of fear."

Sometimes fear is exemplified by resistance. If, when you set your goals, you feel some emotional resistance from yourself, examine it. The achievement of goals is not synonymous with struggle, and you do not have to become emotionally addicted to achievement. But goal-setting and fear-facing give purpose and focus to your invaluable life, and the nature of life is to create, to move freely and purposefully in happiness, to travel from plateau to plateau, gaining knowledge, overcoming obstacles, achieving pride, understanding, and enlightenment.

The easiest way to handle fear is to face it. The failure

to face fear means that you secretly believe the worst is true, and you give great energy when you fear the worst possible outcome of any situation. Fear is magnetic: it attracts more fear. Take heart, though, for courage is magnetic too. Deal with fear and move on.

□ *STEP-BY-STEP TOWARD GOALS* □

What are the very first things you must do to get the show on the road? Write them down. Then proceed to investigate, gather knowledge, tap resources, and obtain advice.

A great feeling of accomplishment is achieved by marking off a step on the way to a goal.

Move on to the next step; go through the process again. Never give up, even in adversity—even when it seems that every atom in the universe is working against you, trying to defeat you.

Reached a plateau yet?

Focus your eyes on the next plateau.

Feel justifiable pride when you reach a plateau. Pat yourself on the back, congratulate your own unique person for this achievement.

Now move on.

Soon it becomes clear that every day you achieve something, every day you move closer to complete success, every day you experience some thrill of victory.

C H A P T E R III

IDENTIFYING YOUR POWER

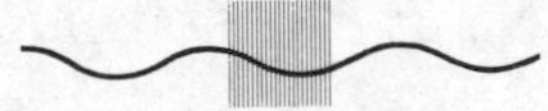

George Bernard Shaw wrote, "One man who has a mind and knows it can always beat ten men who haven't and don't." In the quest for happiness in life—for achievement and accomplishment—once you identify your personal power and bend that power to your will, no obstacle is too large to overcome, no reasonable goal too farfetched. Individual power is awesome in its might.

□ *CHARACTERISTICS OF A POWERFUL PERSON* □

A powerful individual may be the dictator of a small country, the head of a large conglomerate that indiscriminately eats smaller companies, or the man with his finger on the trigger. These offices, of course, are inured with immense power, and the persons who seize and use it this way may be considered "powerful." We don't care to discuss or even consider evil manipulators or common criminals or those who obtain the goodies of life through force or fraud. Ill-gotten gains are ill-gotten gains, and nothing can make a wrong turn into a right.

What we are concerned with is positive personal power,

the power that rightfully belongs to (and indeed is already possessed by) regular folks. The following are some characteristics of a person who has identified and tapped his personal power:

□ KNOWLEDGEABLE. A powerful person has conducted a conscientious program of self-evaluation. He knows himself and his tendencies, his loves and hates, his quirks and faults, his strengths and talents. He has formulated his own philosophy and code of ethics. According to Oliver S. Braston, philosophy is common sense in a dress suit. The powerful person knows that his weaknesses are not fatally debilitating, and that his strengths will not triumph by themselves. He is a human being, and knowledgeable human beings know they are not perfect; we don't own halos. English dramatist Christopher Fry asked, "What, after all, is a halo? It's only one more thing to keep clean." The knowledgeable man does not flog himself repeatedly for his faults; he concentrates on shoring up his strengths. And he never quits evolving, growing, acquiring self-knowledge throughout his life.

□ REASONABLE. The powerful person utilizes reason in all his thought processes. He is guided by reason at all times. Crazy times may *seem* to call for crazy measures, but in the end the reasonable person always wins. When solving a problem or in the midst of a crisis, the powerful person always asks himself, and others if involved, "What is reasonable?" His expectations are reasonable (thereby avoiding unnecessary disappointment). He knows that one does not moisten a stamp with Niagara Falls ("Meaningless Proverb" by P. W. R. Foot).

□ CONFIDENT—HIGH SELF-ESTEEM. The powerful person is confident and sure of his thought processes. He has experimented with decision making, problem-solving, plan making, and other ways and means, and has settled on the processes that work for him. He knows to go back to basics whenever the situation is stymied. He is not a whiner and does not give up or lie down and cry. He doesn't wallow in self-pity. In *The Moon and Sixpence*, W. Somerset Maugham wrote, "The world is quickly bored by the recital of misfortune and willingly avoids the sight of distress." The powerful person does not dwell on misfortune; he calls it baloney and boots it in the bottom.

□ COURAGEOUS. The powerful person is not fearless, but has learned to master fear. He is not deterred by what-ifs and the laughter of knaves. He knows there will be obstacles, barriers, problems, and quandaries, but he does not shrink from the quest for happiness. He knows success is not cheap. He meets with sorrow, and although he may be saddened, he is not KO'd forever. He trusts that time will heal many wounds. Like Sydney J. Harris in *Majority of One*, the powerful person says, "When I hear somebody sigh, 'Life is hard,' I am always tempted to ask, 'Compared to what?' " The powerful person knows that if this round is lost, he'll have another chance in the next one, and defeat in one round doesn't mean complete surrender. Perseverance and stamina will carry him a long way toward victory. Life is not a spectator sport.

□ ASSERTIVE. The powerful person is not belligerent or obnoxious, but he does not demur when he meets opposition. He asserts his values and his beliefs. "Martyrdom is the only way in which a man can become famous without ability," wrote George Bernard Shaw. The powerful person asserts his basic rights to happiness, to strive, to own property, or rise as far as his mind and body will take him, to achieve or not, to love or not, to be a complete human being or not. He does not bow before inferiority, and he does not allow anyone else to rack him back in his perception of self. Eleanor Roosevelt believed that "No one can make you feel inferior without your consent." If you are indecisive, and instead of going back to your tried-and-true basics, you catch yourself mewling, "What do you think I should do?" don't be surprised if someone says, "What difference does it make what *I* think; it's your problem."

□ SENSITIVE. The powerful person does not tread on someone else's feelings in jackboots. There are other human beings who people his world, and some of them are necessary for his happiness. He knows that occasionally another person simply needs a listener, and that if someone confides, he does not necessarily want his problem solved; he may just need to verbalize. Neutral observations are helpful in this situation: "You must be feeling pretty sad." "What a prickly dilemma!" "I am truly sorry for your trouble." "Umm," "Oh, I see," and "Ahh" are good neutral observations. The powerful person does not ignore another's pain, and by the same token, he does not ignore another's success. Bette Midler says that "The worst part of having success is to try finding someone who is happy for you." To withhold praise from one who triumphs is small, and we cannot always be the hero. "Somebody has to sit on the curb and clap as they go by" (Will Rogers).

□ ADAPTABLE. Change is inevitable, and thank God for it! If we reached a certain point and had to stay there, we'd lose the will to live. How terrible if we were doomed forever to circle in a holding pattern over Cincinnati! The powerful person does not fear change, he relishes it. Adaptability to change is exciting, chock-full of opportunities, and offers ever-widening ripples of possibilities. In Maugham's *Of Human Bondage*, the author described a character: "Like all weak men, he laid an exaggerated stress on not changing one's mind." A Taoist teaching encourages the warrior to adapt to his enemy's movements. This is an oriental rule for roll with the punches.

□ HAPPY. If you possess, exercise, understand, strive for, identify, and get a kick out of the above characteristics, you're bound to be happy. There are sure to be times in even the most stalwart warrior's mind when all seems lost. There are times when events appear out of control, times when frantic unfocused energy sprays from us and we deplete ourselves with nothing to show for it. We haven't gained anything from the expenditure of our precious energy: no barriers overcome, no problems solved, no stresses banished, and no tensions eased. Chaos rules. But practice what you have read and believe, go back to basics, and *Do it like you know it*.

□ *EXAMPLES OF PERSONAL POWER* □

Susie was invited to a fancy restaurant for dinner. She'd been to McDonald's but never to Antoine's, and didn't know the proper etiquette. So she did everything in slow motion. She ate slowly and sipped slowly; she cracked lobster claws slowly. Every motion was languid, deliberate, and well thought out. She made it through dinner just fine and had a dreamy time! Her personal power in this situation was channeled into slowing the pace to one she felt comfortable with. She had identified her power even in a strange situation and used it to her advantage.

An IRS audit requires personal power, and the auditee may use his power to come prepared, with all the data and with an attitude of cooperation and courage. Handicapped people must have a tap to their personal power supply—not so much to overcome the handicap, but to deal with others who can't. Other events which require copious amounts of personal power are death or divorce, loss of a job, bankruptcy, drug or alcohol abuse of a loved one, and phobias.

Julie's heart was broken in a love affair when she was very young and immature. She was afraid to seek another romantic relationship because of it, yet she also feared aloneness. If Julie found herself alone, she immediately began to call friends and family or manufacture places to go where there were many other people. She did not like herself enough to enjoy solitude. This dilemma is one many of us have wrestled with; we're afraid to seek intimacy but afraid to be alone. Julie got tired of living in such an uncomfortable situation and she determined to get over it. She began by self-examination, and she identified activities which gave her pleasure while she was alone. Julie discovered that she was really a nice person with good skills and many interests. Now she doesn't dread being by herself; in fact she relishes her time alone. She used her personal power to deal with a personality limitation. Coincidentally, when she reached this healthy point in her emotional growth, the man of her dreams appeared. They'll be married soon.

□ *POWER IS ENERGY* □

When we pray for help from the Father, He sends us a way to tap our own energy. It is up to us to find it and receive it, to employ this energy to achieve the objective we seek. Panic wastes energy. Despair wastes energy. Negative thought and speech waste precious energy. Who in his right mind would deliberately use energy to win something negative—something we don't even like or want!

The person with the energy to move has power. Motive

power. Expending energy to further your desires doesn't make you tired, it stimulates! A person tires easily when all he does is sit flat on his bo-bo and sigh hopeless sighs. Haven't you noticed that when you are engaged in an activity that interests you, how time flies by? If you've got a little cash put together, your bills are paid, and you decide to shop for yourself, why, you've got energy to burn! You could walk around that mall several more times and never feel it!

You call up that energy from somewhere, but where does it come from?

Inside you. Inside your mind and body. And just what is this thing called energy?

It is a paralyzed fact that human beings are made of energy. The universe is made of energy. We live and move in a great energy field. You may remember from high school science that everything, right down to a pebble or a sound, is made of particles which move inside molecules. These little gems orbit around each other at different speeds—they vibrate. Sound moves along on waves. Light also. Electricity surges around, passing positive and negative charges from one particle to another. You can even see heat waves as they shimmer upward from the earth in a mirage. These energies are speed demons, but they are "fine," not "dense." Blood is made of corpuscles and cells that travel through our bodies, building here, healing there. A rock, now, is made of energy which is plenty dense. It moves not at all; at least it doesn't to the human eye. But the rock's particles do move; they just move ever so slowly. The brain can hardly comprehend so much activity going on around us! There must be infinite energy in the universe, and wouldn't it be swell to tap into this energy! Just like charity, personal energy-tapping begins at home.

Energy outside and inside the mind and body vibrates at different rates, and it is the difference in vibratory rates which affects perception. All forms of energy are related, from the finer energies like thought and light to the denser energies like rocks and wood. God is the source of all energy and when He created His children, He designed their bodies to produce all the energy needed for a long, long time. Personal energy is continually replaced. Elementary science taught us that energy is never destroyed; it simply changes its form.

Our goal here is to help you identify the power energy which lies within you.

You can parade through life glowing in the dark like safety orange paint or Day-Glo yellow. You can do it. Yes, you can. All you must do is take responsibility for your life and live it according to your own plan. Channel your energy, both mental and physical. Surely everyone is familiar with the adage about marching to the beat of a different drummer. Listen to your own beat. Your drummer may be Gene Krupa or Alex Van Halen, but both will power you onward.

Young Brian runs track in high school and he's just beginning to find his coordination. The open quarter or 400-meter run is a tough race because the runner must dash full-out for a long distance. Brian hears a drumbeat in his head as he runs. He concentrates on nothing but the beat and he speeds up the beat as he goes along, so he is always accelerating. His shortness of breath doesn't matter, his burning calf muscles don't bother him, sweat in his eyes doesn't slow him down. He just keeps running to the beat. The finish line is always a surprise! Terrific physical labor is nothing when the mind takes over.

Christy also runs track in high school. She is a great sprinter. As she warms up at the starting line, just before she steps into the blocks, her eyes fix with unwavering intensity on the string at the finish line. She focuses all her energy there and announces to herself that she *must* be the first to snap that string. As she runs, her eyes never move;

that string is the only thing in the world. As she nears the string, she dips her upper body forward, almost like bowing to her own greatness. Very few have beaten her.

These are examples of mind energy connecting with physical energy. Is it becoming clear that mind power is awesome power? Even if you cannot see it? The way to begin channeling your thought energy to power your physical self is ridiculously uncomplicated. Just decide to do it. Simply say yes, I will. Not only can energy be used to accomplish new goals, it can be used to stop undesirable habits. Again, all you have to do is decide.

If you remember nothing else from this book, remember this: There comes a time in your life when your permission must be obtained for evil to be done to you. Realize that you can put a stop to this outrage by pronouncing one word. The word is no. Ayn Rand, the controversial philosopher/novelist, gave us this priceless gift. We have the power energy to say no! By the same premise, there comes a time when your permission must be obtained so that you may succeed. Realize that you can succeed by pronouncing one word. The word is yes.

You have the power to say no and yes. You have the power and the responsibility to live your life fully or have your life live you. You can be bounced around by another's energy; you can be blown every which way on the winds of another's whim; you can be beaten and stopped in your quest for success by any energy. *If you allow it.*

Or you can use your power to say yes. Yes to responsibility and yes to happiness. You can speak positively and look forward eagerly to the opportunities that await you. You can stand proudly among your fellows and know, in the deepest recesses of your being, that you have the necessary power and energy within yourself for whatever need you have, that you can achieve any goal you desire if you have commitment, a plan, and if you harness your personal power, focused and channeled, to accomplish your goals.

You can free yourself from the old chains that bind you. Using personal power energy can break those chains and grant you liberty. "Liberty means responsibility. That is why most men dread it." George Bernard Shaw wrote that in Maxims for Revolutionists.

We *are* revolutionists. We are revolting against "old tapes," against the Without Syndrome and the Thwart Monster, and against the heavy burden of our unhappiness. What a chore to travel through life with mud clinging to our boots—the heavy, clay mud of unhappiness weighs many pounds—and our clothes smell nasty from guilt and the lies we've told, and the half-dishonorable compromises we've made. Scrape the mud from your boots and resurrect the lighthearted spirit inside.

Human beings were not placed on this earth to lead a passive existence. We are doers: consciousness in physical bodies built for action. We are not meant to be bowed by the weight of life. Our posture is upright. We face a life full of exciting possibilities.

You have it, this personal power. You are in charge of the vast reservoir of energy churning inside your body and your mind. You direct the use of your energy, outwardly and inwardly. You control. You direct. You act. Feel the hot lava of power bubbling inside, waiting to move, waiting to push you forward and upward. Be still and feel your power.

□ *ENERGY IS MAGNETIC* □

"Matter" is vibrating energy, and there are many other kinds of energy and each is magnetic: light and atomic energy, creative and mental energy, electricity. A basic law of science is: energy of a certain quality or vibration tends to attract energy of a similar quality or vibration.

This concept is mysterious to those of us who are not well versed in physics and other sciences, but some basic truths are self-evident. The English poet Ralph Hodgson tells us that "Some things have to be believed to be seen," and energy is just such a force. If we accept the premise that all is energy, we can understand that it is magnetic—energy attracts a like energy. Positive and negative forces magnetize. Little magnets cling to the refrigerator door; energy forces attract one another.

When I say, "I'm tired today," my mind hears and my body adjusts to feel fatigue. When I say, "I slept well," my mind hears and my body adjusts to exhibit vitality. If I whine about my troubles and about how others take advantage of poor little me, that belief will manifest itself in my life with a vengeance. If I affirm my own special qualities and see myself full of light and strength, my mind and body are flooded with good feelings, I smile, my spine straightens. I feel mighty, in control, and very, very capable. I possess magnetic power. I feel powerful, so I attract power. I feel strong, so I attract strength.

To live successfully, you must think and act. To think is an act of choice, and you choose the content of your thoughts. Old-timers say that even the man who can't make a choice has made a choice. Every activity, every behavior, every event, every emotion, begins with thought. Every great achievement begins with thought. Every great idea and invention, every great love, begins with thought. Thought is an energy.

□ *THOUGHT ENERGY* □

You can summon any energy in any amount that you want or need at any time. Fantastic feats of courage and physical strength have been performed simply by an individual summoning, from inside himself, the personal energy and power needed to perform the deed. Remember the frail grandmother who lifted an automobile off her grandson . . . the soldier who carried his buddy miles in the rice paddies to get medical help . . . superhuman rescue efforts in earthquakes or avalanches. All these examples show that human beings have within themselves a huge warehouse of power which ordinarily is never utilized until a time of crisis. Can we not identify this warehouse and call upon it when we *want* to? Of course. All that is needed is skill, knowledge, and the willingness to accept and wield personal power.

Here's another thought-provoking question. Have you ever considered the spoken word as a powerful energy?

□ *SPOKEN WORD ENERGY* □

Recognizing the power of the spoken word will help identify your personal power. Some adages are true: the words you send out into the universe will return to you tenfold. Curses, like chickens, come home to roost. The saddest words of tongue or pen are these four words: what might have been. More pain has been inflicted with words than has ever been with swords. More joy has been given with words than ever was with gold.

An essential need all humans and animals possess is the need to communicate. Verbal communication is the highest form of communication. It is the most efficient and the most powerful. When we deal with words, we deal with dynamite; be careful what you say.

The spoken word drives thoughts and images into our conscious and subconscious mind and the conscious and subconscious minds of others. You are free to say whatever you wish, but you are responsible for the benefits or the disasters those words reap. Mothers admonish their children: "If you can't say something nice, don't say anything at all." Think before you speak and remember that it's hard to put a foot in a shut mouth.

You choose the words you send into the universe. You command mighty power with the spoken word. You can change your life and your circumstances by simply speaking the words. New Age author, the late Frances Scovell Shinn, believed that "Your word is your wand." Relish the challenge of speaking positively, with precision, with force and commitment, all the time. You can speak the language of happiness and thereby attract happiness into your life.

How lovely it is to hear words of admiration, love, inspiration. How dreary to hear despair, sorrow, self-pity. How we love to hear someone sing praise and be thankful; words of tender regard and exultation are the sweetest music! But words of doom and dread turn us away from the speaker. We do not enjoy complainers and gripers. So, be mindful of the words you say.

Let's put this verbal energy to work.

CHAPTER IV

AFFIRMATIONS AND VISUALIZATIONS

Affirmations are powerful, positive statements of belief. The key words are "powerful," "positive," and "belief." We've talked about power and we know now where it is: inside ourselves. Positive is simply the opposite of negative, and for our purposes, "positive" is the only way to fly. "Belief" is another story.

□ *BELIEF* □

Remember when Tinker Bell in *Peter Pan* was dying, when her light grew dimmer and dimmer? Peter Pan called upon all the children of the world to clap their hands and say, "I believe!" This childlike promise of belief saved Tinker's life, and her light grew stronger and brighter. This fairy tale is dear to everyone, and we suspect that one reason is the assurance that our belief (and the acting out of that unshakable belief) somehow makes a positive difference in the great scheme of things.

Rock-solid belief in ourselves and our abilities grants us an immovable foundation from which to grow. We must, however, know every intimate, minute corner of that foundation. We must know and love ourselves. In the end, each one of us will have trod his own path, and we will have traversed it alone. This task is not as spooky as it appears because if you believe in yourself and like who you are, being *by* yourself holds no threat. In the end, man stands alone in his holy temple, and he must let nothing defile it. In the end, we will face whatever force is stronger than ourselves, *by* ourselves. It behooves us, then, to construct a foundation based on beliefs and a code of actions which intensify its strength.

As a simple exercise, begin a positive sentence: "I believe I am . . ." and see what follows. What follows should be the unadulterated truth. "I believe I am a good teacher" or "a good painter" or "a good listener." How does it make you feel? If your positive statement is indeed the truth, it makes you feel pretty proud, doesn't it? Take a few minutes and ferret out a few of those beliefs and verbalize them. Consider your choices and note the way your head automatically rises and how your lips are touched with a slight smile of wonder. Brick that positive belief with the mortar of truth into your foundation.

Search out those things about yourself that make you proud of who you are. Block by block, stone upon stone, construct a foundation of belief in your mind, because, as usual . . .

□ *IT ALL BEGINS IN THE MIND* □

Your mind creates your reality. How we respond to certain stimuli, how we feel about certain ideals, and what moves us emotionally, it all begins in the mind. With lightning-fast speed, the mind receives and interprets thought energy on many levels simultaneously. With a vast battery of power at its beck and call, the mind is constantly at work.

Sometimes the mind follows the same patterns of interpretation simply because it has been conditioned to follow the same pattern ("old tapes" again). These patterns can be changed like the course of a river. If a river eats away at its banks, and with a flood of force behind it threatens livestock and property, man in his wisdom can dam that river and direct it on a different course. In other words, what the mind creates, the mind can change. Hallelujah! Now we know! Now we know that regardless of what conditioning we've had in the past, regardless of the muck and mire we've slogged through mentally and emotionally, regardless of our appearances, we *can* alter patterns of thinking. We *can* overcome history, and as Oscar Wilde wrote in 1890, "The one duty we have to history is to rewrite it."

If every time you see your husband chatting with a beautiful babe, your jealous cobra-thought rears its ugly head, *that* is conditioning. If, when faced with your child's temper tantrum, you immediately begin shouting and swatting, *that* is a patterned response. One of the authors experienced an odd pattern response with her former husband: every time they were to leave on a trip, the husband became irritable, snappish, and downright rude. Every vacation or business trip began with this scenario. When they got to the bottom of it, they found that the husband had been conditioned to act this way because his parents demonstrated the same responses years before. The trips were different, the participants were different, and the time period was different—but his patterned response was the same. Curiouser and curiouser.

Terry, a young law student, experienced test anxiety. This is a common enough phenomenon but crippling just the same. He overcame his panic before an examination by admitting his anxiety, noting its unreasonableness and consciously resolving to destroy the patterned response and replace it with a new one. (Incidentally, he passed the Bar.) Text anxiety and many other patterned responses are just not reasonable. With tongue in cheek, Oscar Wilde, in *The Picture of Dorian Gray*, declaimed, "I can stand brute force, but brute reason is quite unreasonable. There is something unfair about its use. It is hitting below the intellect."

Isn't this amazing? What the mind can create, the mind can change! Are you getting a sneaky feeling that some of the calamities which befall us may be caused by *ourselves*?

□ *OVERCOMING THE SELF-LIMITING MIND-SET* □

Nathaniel Branden, in *Honoring the Self*, explains that "The greatest barrier to achievement and success is not lack of talent or ability but, rather, the fact that achievement and success, above a certain level, are outside our self-concept, our image of who we are and what is appropriate to us. The greatest barrier to love is the secret fear that we are unlovable. The greatest barrier to happiness is the wordless sense that happiness is not our proper destiny." What a mouthful!

This scathingly true philosophy is really scary. What if it's true? What if we unintentionally (or intentionally—let's be honest) sabotage ourselves? What if we ambush our own happiness and success because to do so is our conditioned or patterned response? Do we lie in wait in the bushes just as the lion stalks the gazelle, savaging our own efforts toward happiness?

You will sometimes hear old-timers intone, "Well, when I was a pup, we *never* . . ." did such and so. Or "*I* was raised that a person *always* . . ." did this and that. Sometimes, and more times than we consciously recognize, we limit success by the ideas we bring with us from childhood. These mind-sets are baggage we haul into our adult lives, and they color our responses in mischievous ways. We can be severely limited by them. How many times have you said, with a horrified look on your face, "My God, I sound just like my mother!"

Other ideas from childhood are positive and urge us onward and upward, but we'll concentrate here on those mind-sets which are potentially damaging.

Selfishness is bad. Children should be seen and not heard. Always respect your elders. Never contradict an older person. We have discovered that some of these maxims not only hinder our children's emotional development, but some instructions are downright physically dangerous. Think about how many missing children are out there somewhere because they were taught never to question the actions of an adult. And let's face it, some adults are not worthy of respect, either from other adults or from children. In most cases, selfishness is not bad; in other cases, it can be destructive. Children have valid feelings just like adults, and it promotes self-confidence when adults actually value their children's thoughts and ideas. Let's not nip creativity in the bud by shushing our kids every time they open their mouths.

Some proverbs we learned in childhood are invaluable. Never run with the scissors. Always whittle away from yourself. Don't take candy from strangers. As we grow into adulthood and our life experiences widen and pile up, we can disseminate this information, choose what advice we can apply, and throw away the bad stuff like chaff in the wind.

It is difficult to find out what limits us and why. Maybe we limit ourselves because we have been conditioned over a period of time, even as adults. Consider a destructive relationship or career. The battered wife has been conditioned to believe that her partner's abusive behavior is acceptable. The promiscuous man thinks being called a stud is admirable.

Whatever mind-set is limiting your success, screw your courage to the sticking place and face your baggage. Identify it, proceed to pack it up, and throw it away.

To identify the self-limiting barrier, admit it and verbalize it. Say, "I seem to attract the wrong kind of partner—one who treats me badly." Speak the words, "I never complete a task because I'm frightened of the possible result of my success." "I don't love because I'm afraid of being hurt." Don't gnash your teeth and bewail your situation, but state it in a businesslike manner. And never say these limiting statements again, either out loud or in your mind. Period.

Understand that you *can* change a mind-set. Some unseen force is not magnetizing you to attract partners who are bad for you, those who do not enhance your life but cause you pain. You are subconsciously drawn to them and they to you. But you can change that belief. You *can* attract partners who bring excitement, knowledge, compassion, and understanding to your life.

You hate your job, you hate the people you work with, your job is demeaning and low-paying. Why can't you move on to something else? "I can't get another job" . . . and yah-yah-yah and whine-whine-whine. You *can* do something about your career, and it is your responsibility to take the corrective action; that is, if you want to be happy in your work.

The following statements are carved-in-marble facts: You *always* have a choice, for even not to decide is making a choice. You are never trapped, at least not for very long, and you can always find an escape. You choose "bad" things and you choose "good" things for your life. You seek disasters as well as triumphs.

Cut the next paragraph out of this book and tape it to

your mirror, carry it in your wallet, or slip it in your top desk drawer.

You can change the quality of your life. You can identify your power and your limiting beliefs, and you can use that power to banish limitations. *You choose. You decide.* You can choose whether or not you want to be happy. Don't curse the universe or others for where you are this day. YOU put yourself there. Command your potential for achievement and use the tools you were given to weave dignity, integrity, honor, and happiness into the fabric of your life. Take action! NOW!

□ *HOW?* □

Break a mind-set by chipping away at it little by little. Important questions to ask yourself when you confront a patterned response will reveal startling answers: "Just how important is this?" "Who owns the problem?" "Who is in charge of this?" "What do I want to do?" "What is reasonable?" "Am I looking for negativity—anticipating problems which may or may not occur?" "Am I wasting energy in a no-win situation?"

John is the most frustrated man you'd ever care to meet. His romantic relationships always fell in a heap just when they looked most promising. John had some unreasonable, illogical preconceptions about love relationships. He thought love was magic and cured all ills and healed all wounds and automatically made the future bright forever. John would meet a woman, become attracted to her, have some fun times with her, then begin making long-term plans. He would dream that they'd have a little house and a little garden, and they'd go dancing, and the romance would always be exactly like the infatuation they felt for one another at the beginning. John told all of this to his ladylove over and over. But, alas, the woman would move on, gently advising John that a big-time commitment just wasn't in the stars. John, of course, would drag around heartbroken for a while . . . until the next wonderful woman strolled along.

What's wrong with this picture?

1. Love is not magic.
2. Love will not cure all ills.
3. Love will not heal all wounds.
4. Love does not make the future automatically bright forever.
5. Attraction is not love.
6. Fun times do not a strong foundation make.
7. Infatuation doesn't last.

Playwright Max Kauffmann never knew what happiness in love was ". . . until I got married. And by then it was too late." Did John have unreasonable and illogical expectations? You may be scoffing at poor John right this minute, thinking what a fool this guy is or that anybody knows better than this schmuck. But haven't you—if only for a little while—been so enchanted with another human being that you just knew it was going to last forever and it would be the most wonderful, extraordinary love affair in the history of man?

Chip away at that mind-set, John, and you'll be happier in the long run. Don't look at every woman as a potential long-term, commitment-ready partner. Don't talk yourself into being handed a train ticket home. Relax. Find yourself a reasonable, logical mind-set with which to evaluate your romantic relationships. You'll probably avoid some pain as well.

John, say this: "I am a romantic fool and I really don't want a fantasy relationship. I want a relationship which is real and lasting and loving. I want a reasonable, logical partner to share my life with, one who will love me and one whom I can love. I choose not to be disappointed in love relationships from this day forward."

Disappointment comes from failed expectations. Depression follows, then despair, and finally surrender. A failed expectation, if you cling to it unreasonably, is a tar baby: it is dark and dreary and feels like running in quicksand. Once you set unreasonable, illogical goals or believe in illogical, unreasonable expectations, you are doomed to repeat the disappointment/surrender spiral. The Thwart Monster gleefully invades your life and colors everything in it with a murky brush. Then, once again, you suffer from the Without Syndrome.

When you destroy destructive mind-sets, shining opportunities spring up. And the great thing about these opportunities is that they are real and achievable and attainable. Once John gets his mind right, look for him to find happiness with a reasonable, logical partner and accomplish reasonable, logical goals.

Now it is clear that we can fade destructive mind-sets and break down self-limiting barriers. What's next?

□ *CREATING A NEW REALITY* □

Use the motivation and goal-setting chapters and the information about self-limiting concepts to build a new reality with your mind. Be guided by reason, logic, high self-esteem, your native intelligence, intuition, and talents. Use your imagination to create a real life, one filled with happiness and satisfaction. A fulfilled happy life consists of enjoyable work—and any work is creative and satisfying when done with a thinking mind, freedom to think and to own the product of your creativity, enough money and food, shelter, communication, love, and any other thing you can think of which makes you feel happy. You can have all that and more. Yes, you can. If you can visualize it in your mind and use the energies described in previous chapters to make it happen.

Hold on a minute. Visualize?

□ *VISUALIZING* □

Essential in the program of creating your new reality is the art of visualization. This is a mental process governed by the reasoning, conscious mind. Visualizing is not the same as visioning, which is a spiritual process prompted by intuition. Much has been written recently about creative visualization, and much has been achieved by individuals who have learned this skill.

Human beings see pictures in the mind almost constantly; it is such an integral part of day-to-day functioning that we forget it is happening. When we take control of it and program the pictures deliberately, we are one step closer to achieving goals.

Use all the senses to learn the skill of visualization: sight, sound, smell, touch, taste, and intuition. All the information channeled from the senses travels immediately to the brain where the intricate, delicate process of thinking, reasoning, and integrating knowledge into our experience takes place. Use memories from the past. As a matter of fact, we'll use experiences from the past to learn visualization for the future.

☐ *BEGINNING EXERCISE* ☐

From your past experiences, identify a specific cherished time or event. For instance: intimacy is a treasured memory, and you should locate in your mind's eye an intimate moment that you have experienced—just a scene—and relive it again in your mind using the senses.

Artemio tells of a wonderful memory when he was a little boy and his dad took him fishing:

"I remember the hot summer sun . . . how it beamed down and made my hair hot . . . how it gave texture and brilliance to trees, grass, and water. I remember the sky, how blue and clear, dotted with wispy clouds—a soft breeze moved those clouds around—and I squinted my eyes when I looked up into the sky. The air was aromatic with pine scent from the evergreens, with an undercurrent of that particular fishy-bait smell. Last night's campfire still smoldered and that distinctive odor floated softly in the air. I can still feel the cane pole in my grimy little hands and see drops of sparkling water chasing one another down the fishing line. My dad's big hands seemed enormous as they helped me bait the hook. He needed a shave but his scratchy face felt wonderful as he rubbed his cheek against mine. Cool mud squished up delightfully through my toes at the edge of the pond. My cork plopped into the water, and, in a moment, Dad's soft voice whispered, 'You've got a bite.' I was fearful, full of anticipation and suppressed excitement; we watched that cork so closely . . . it twitched . . . and twitched again. Dad said, 'Wait, Artemio, just a little longer. *Now!* Jerk that pole out of the water!' My fish was a tiny perch, a rainbow-colored shining thing! It flipped and turned on my line. My dad congratulated me on my fisherman's skill, and I remember how satisfied and comforted I was when we gently unhooked the prize and slipped him back into the cool water, back to his home in the pond."

Artemio called up every sensory perception he could to savor this memory; he could smell the smells, see the beauty, feel the emotions. This is the process.

Look deeply at your life experiences and consciously identify feelings and sensings. Relive them and remember them with crystal clarity in your mind. File this information away; you'll need it later as you use creative visualization to actualize your success for the future.

Be conscious also of events as they unfold in the present. Heighten your awareness of how things smell, how they look and feel, the texture of things, both the beautiful and the beastly. Make it a practice to identify these sensings and note the responses brought about by them. Not only will you enjoy the present more fully if you consciously recognize the sense of the moment, but your future memories will be much clearer and more enjoyable.

□ *CREATING YOUR OWN VISUALIZATIONS* □

Begin thinking about change, for change is what we seek in creative visualization. Think about how you would like a future event to turn out or how you want a relationship to change.

Use your senses to imagine the desired situation.

Suppose you want to lose weight. See yourself, in your mind, slender and feeling good, head held high. Don't just see yourself skinny; see a situation or a scene in which you look wonderfully slim: you're waiting for a bus. There's a nip in the air, not enough for a sweater, but a crisp, clean feeling in the breeze. The sky is a brilliant clear blue and street sounds float around you. Your skirt is blue gabardine and your blouse is creamy silk. Everything fits perfectly—not too tight in the waist—and you see no bulges or spare tires. Your stomach is flat! Why, an ice skater's stomach is not any flatter than yours! Toss that head and gaze about you as you wait for the bus, and when the bus arrives, see yourself moving easily up the steps and walking (without turning sideways) down the aisle to a seat. See others look admiringly at your figure. It pleases them to see a lovely woman with a lovely form. You don't breathe heavily. You sit comfortably. This is a scrumptious scene!

Now think about how you *feel* about being so beautiful. You're proud, of course. You are confidence personified. The air caresses you, voices alert you, your senses are alive and functioning at full potential.

□ *IMAGINATION!* □

Creative visualization is the technique of using your imagination to create what you want in your life. It is the ability to create a picture in your mind, focus all your positive energy upon it, and direct the flow of positive energy to develop the picture.

Paint your mental picture completely, right down to the threads of fabric that clothe you. Let your imagination take flight and open up this fanciful portion of your mind to opportunities and possibilities; you can imagine anything you want. You can also alter your picture in any manner until it appears perfect in every detail. When the authors were outlining this book, we saw reams and reams of research notes. We saw the book on display in our favorite bookstore. We saw the check from the publishing company. Our imaginations pictured our success, and it is becoming a reality.

□ *CAUTION* □

Make sure that what you image is truly what you want. Do you *really* want all the money in the world? Or do you just want enough? Do you simply desire the perfect amount at the perfect time? Be prepared to receive what you *expect* to receive, because we do reap what we sow, and we do receive the triumphs or disasters we seek.

It is said that intuition is the Father whispering messages to us. Don't be afraid to trust your own intuition—your personal message from the Father. Bob Dylan cautioned us, in an old song, not to become slaves to what someone else believed, but to trust in ourselves. Act on the Father's advice.

Another word of caution: When you creatively visualize, positively *do not* entertain any negative thoughts. Whenever you think a negative thought or create a negative picture, immediately cancel it out with a positive one. Consciously push out any thoughts about what you might lose and think only of what can be gained.

Don't play what-if with yourself. Ninety-eight percent of the bugaboos we worry about never happen. So don't hunt trouble or look for pitfalls on the journey to success. Stamp indelibly on your mind a mental picture of yourself as succeeding and keep it bright and fresh. Banish doubts and sweep away anxiety. March forward courageously, keeping your visualization fresh and clear, toward your goal.

Don't play if-only. Don't play I-have-no-choice or not-yet. These are disguises worn by the Thwart Monster. Defeat the nasty Thwart Monster in whatever mask he wears and get on with creative positive visualization.

□ *AFFIRM YOUR VISUALIZATION* □

Always wrap up your visualizing sessions with an affirmation. The spoken affirmation of a successful reality drives more securely into the conscious and subconscious mind the mental picture we seek to develop.

Just as your mental imaging should be structured, so should the affirmation that confirms it. While channeling positive creative energy into a sharply definitive mind image, the words of the affirmation must be powerful, vivid, and evoke an instant emotional response.

Have there been scenes in movies or books or real life which evoked an immediate response or struck a chord of recognition inside you? Conjure up some of those scenes and consider them. For example, in television's "The Burning Bed," Farrah Fawcett's terror brings bile to the throat at the unbelievable horror of her husband's abuse; a rush of sweet love accompanies Jimmy Stewart as he runs home to his family for Christmas in *It's a Wonderful Life;* the aroma and chill of a misty Scottish moor in a historical romance novel.

Merle pinpoints this feeling exactly when she recalls the night her twelve-year-old daughter won the World Champion saddle for the American Junior Rodeo Association's barrel-racing event. Merle says she'll never forget that night or any of the night's tiniest, most insignificant details. Her daughter wore pink, and the smell of horses and leather and dust filled the indoor arena. The crowd was huge; all the competitors and their parents and friends were there, plus the spectators who always turn out en masse for a West Texas rodeo. The lights dimmed and people got still. The announcer's voice boomed into the coliseum as this tiny little girl trudged to the middle of the dirt arena to accept the brand-new saddle and the title of World's Champion.

These supercharged responses possess the intensity we seek to affirm our new reality. This intensity can be evoked not only from past experience, but for future desires. We can obtain this intensity of mind-force by the use of certain words and phrases put together in affirmative form.

In composing good affirmations, use picture words, power verbs, and phrases which evoke instant responses. Consider, one by one, these words and the response they evoke in you:

SIZZLE	GLITTER
RAZOR-SHARP	DISSOLVE
HONOR	TRIUMPH
DOORS FLY OPEN	OBSTACLES MELT
RADIATE	DYNAMITE
STACKS AND STACKS	BANISH
WILLOWY	STEADFAST
EFFORTLESSLY	ABUNDANCE

□ *DOs AND DON'Ts* □

In composing affirmations, when you feel the tendency to use a to-be verb, kill it. To-be verbs dilute the power. Use descriptive, explosive words—verbs with movement and force. Notice the difference in these two statements:

"I AM ABLE TO COMPLETE TASKS."

"I COMPLETE TASKS QUICKLY AND EFFICIENTLY."

Do use colorful nouns. Remember that OBSTRUCTION is more colorful than PROBLEM.

Stay in the active voice.

Don't say, "I WILL HANDLE STRESS AT WORK." Do say, "I AM COMPETENT AND CAPABLE AT WORK."

Don't say, "I WILL TRY TO MAKE AN A PLUS ON MY TEST AT SCHOOL." Do say, "I SAIL EFFORTLESSLY THROUGH MY

EXAMINATION, IMMEDIATELY RECALLING DETAILS AND INFORMATION STORED IN MY RAZOR-SHARP BRAIN."

'Nuff said.

□ *BEGIN WITH THANKS* □

Begin your affirmations with thanks. Acknowledge with gratitude the blessings of your life and remember that you have more power to call upon than you thought. Through the Father and with His grace, you possess the ability to achieve greatness. So, begin your affirmations, "Thank you, Father . . ." It brings to the forefront of the mind that the Kingdom is yours.

A beautiful phrase of thanks is found in the Episcopal Book of Common Prayer: "FATHER, YOU ARE THE GIVER OF EVERY GOOD AND PERFECT GIFT." To begin with thanks reminds us that our strength is the strength of the Father, in His light we see light, and in His path we do not stumble.

Another reason to begin with gratitude is that it solidifies the belief that everything we want and need is taking place in the present—right now—and that we are already receiving what we affirm. This validates and reinforces the creative visualization.

□ *THE ALL-POWERFUL VOICE* □

By your words you will live and by your words you will perish. So be careful of words and how you deliver them. Your voice is powerful, so use it well.

As you deliver your affirmations out loud, your voice should be firm with unshakable belief. Socrates said, "It is well to affirm your own truth," and that true belief should be stated with conviction and commitment in your voice. Each word of your affirmation should be spoken slowly and enunciated precisely. Contemplate each word and phrase in your mind as you speak.

The rate should be slow. Don't drag the pace, but savor the words and phrases and measure them out. Relish the images the words evoke.

Even in casual conversation, negative words attract negative situations. Avoid negativity in any of its forms. If your voice begins to whine, close it up right quick, and don't open it again until it sounds positive and firm. If you must think and speak a negative word, speak and think of it as dissolving or dissipating, being swept away or banished.

This program ought to be performed in private, so if a booming voice is required, boom out. When tenderness is called for, a gentle tone enhances the visualization. You are in charge of your voice and of the words it utters. Use it for positive purposes.

CHAPTER V

COLOR ENERGY

Color energy is another power that is available right at our fingertips. We take this energy for granted, but we should never forget how it beautifies our world. This resource is more than mere beauty, however. It embodies a positive force which is vital to our happiness and success.

Color is a mode of light vibration, and a vibration of light is a quivering motion of energy at a certain rate. Light is luminous radiant energy and all matter continuously emits it.

Pure color in light can be identified when a sunbeam shines through a prism. Sir Isaac Newton discovered the color spectrum in 1672, and he identified seven colors—the colors of the rainbow: violet, indigo, blue, green, yellow, orange, and red. For three centuries, these colors were the only ones that were considered "real." The authors theorize that a rainbow after a storm is the earth's aura, washed fresh and clean, with all the beautiful colors set out for us to appreciate. Crowned with the lovely rainbow, the world is in balance.

The whole planet, from the oceans, minerals, and plants, to animals and human beings, is dependent upon light and its amazing properties for existence. The air we breathe is permeated with light and color. As such, color is a force of immeasurable power. Color is energy; therefore, color is magnetic!

While we appreciate color and its beauty, we can also consciously and deliberately change our lives and our health by utilizing . . .

□ *BASIC COLOR KNOWLEDGE* □

Each color-energy ray vibrates at a different frequency, and colors work both independently and together. It is present and active in our bodies, internally and externally, physically and mentally. Since everything in the universe is differentiated basically by the rate at which its particles vibrate, and every vibrating wavelength is magnetic, it follows that wavelengths affect one another. Magnetic waves are absorbed into the body or repelled by it; these waves promote balance or disharmony.

Some color wavelengths are short, like violet. The longest wavelength is red. Red rays vibrate slowly and emit a "heavier" energy; violet rays move fast, therefore radiating a lighter energy. Green is smack in the center of the spectrum and represents the middle ground, a balance.

The combination of colors of the spectrum produce an infinite variety of colors. Purple is made from a mix of red and blue. Green is produced from blue and yellow, and orange is a combination of yellow and red.

White light contains all light, the entire spectrum. Black is the absence of light or the total absorption of color. Both black and white, as absolutes, are not really "colors" although they traditionally evoke definite opinions.

Socially and culturally, black and white have no consistent interpretation. In some societies, white suggests purity and black represents evil. In other cultures, white is the bad guy and black symbolizes reverence and piety.

Mourners at American funerals tend to wear black, although this practice has fallen into disuse in the past decade. In China, however, mourners wear white, the caskets are white, and white is the appropriate color for funeral flowers. The pope wears white; some priests wear black. Members of other religious orders wear black *and* white.

Some Native American tribes considered the color black a powerful talisman. Black was worn in battle because it made the warrior invulnerable. Then there is the legend of the white buffalo, whose hide promised great curative power when stroked. In some oriental societies, black and white together signified duality—man and woman—perfect harmony between opposites.

White and black also have racial meanings, familiarly depicted by the white "race" and the "black" race in conflict. The human race as a whole has good cause to be horrified at the pain inflicted in the name of "race." After all, it is simply the difference in skin color, and when we stop to consider how ridiculous that differentiation is, most of us have the grace to look properly ashamed.

Actually, races are alike in thousands of ways and different only in a few. All men are one race, one species, and as one wise man said, ". . . skin color can be very distinctive, but a man's skin color is no more important than the shape of his toes."

Pastel colors contain large amounts of white pigment. Tints also contain white. Tones are colors that contain gray, and shades are colors that contain black.

Color wavelengths are also separated into octaves. An example is rose which is the higher octave of red. While red is passion, rose provides a gentler version of passion, such as tender regard and sweet affection.

Human beings see color, hear color, and feel color. You'll find this is true if you blindfold yourself and touch a black cloth and then a white cloth in the sunlight. If you concentrate hard enough and channel that concentration to the tactile sense, you can even distinguish between red and blue, orange and violet.

Music has color too. Consider the "blues." Hot jazz is red and lullabies are soft violet. Children's songs are yellow and Sousa marches are orange. Close your eyes the next time you listen to your favorite music, and see if you can identify its color.

Music affects human beings, but color probably affects us most intrinsically of all.

□ *HOW COLOR AFFECTS US* □

Colors produce mental, physical, emotional, and spiritual responses. These responses are divided into three parts. *Restful* colors produce a quiet and passive feeling and enhance contemplation and reflection. *Revitalizing* colors create conditions of change and expansion; these colors encourage improvement and balance. *Stimulating* colors inspire and excite feelings of activity, ambition, and desire.

In recent years, scientists have studied the effects color has on us. Color can be used in many ways, either subtly or flamboyantly, to achieve a desired atmosphere, to promote growth and health, and to exert certain influences on human beings.

Hospitals downplay negative aspects by decorating with soothing colors like pale green and cream, or yellows and bright reds and oranges in the children's wing. Hospitals for the mentally disturbed would never use blazing red or murky gray. Color energy evokes a passive response or an active one, with many levels in between. Basically the red end of the spectrum stimulates while the blue end calms.

On a simple, more basic level, consider these examples: if I were sad (and wanted to be happy), I would not consciously choose to wear black. I would clothe myself in warm, exciting red, and I would respond to bright sunshine yellow in a positive manner. After a day of stress at work, I would welcome a quiet place decorated in gentle blue . . . the caressing blue of the ocean. If I were anxious and fragmented emotionally, I would seek the balancing effects of the healthy green of spring grass. Color energies can promote balance and harmony.

□ *HARMONY* □

Physical, mental, emotional, and spiritual health can be helped or hindered by the use of wonderful color energy rays. The highest achievement, of course, is harmony—harmony between the body, mind, spirit, and the universe. This state epitomizes optimum good health.

Harmony depicts the alignment of the forces of the universe with the inner energy of man. When cosmic energy is aligned or "attuned" with the body, perfect harmony is achieved, at least as far as human beings are concerned. When we are balanced and harmonious, we discover how powerful we really are. The crackling electric energy of the universe dances around us.

The use of color energy rays coupled with the power of the mind is one path to perfect harmony; this combination produces enlightenment, knowledge, and personal power!

Is your understanding of color energy becoming clearer? It is exciting to discover how color influences us, and how we can use color to create dramatic changes in our lives. Color energy coupled with personal power—this is getting good!

Let's examine each color of the spectrum and the facets of life it affects.

□ *BRIGHT RED* □

In comparison with colors at the opposite end of the spectrum, Red emits a somewhat coarse energy. It generally represents passion, strength, conquest, vigor, action, vitality, and the power of life. Red affects the physical nature on its most basic levels.

Clear Red is exciting, and its purpose is to experience, to express, to accomplish, and to reach goals. It has ambition, and it is the fuel for creativity. This warm color drives and challenges and prepares us for adventure.

The pulsing vitality provided by Red color energy enriches life. It intensifies self-expression by clarifying the outward and visible signs of an inward motivation. Red is the single most-used color in patriotic flags because it makes such a bold, definite statement. Native sons rise as one behind their country's banner emblazoned in Red.

In the glow of sparkling Red, the goal-oriented person finds fuel to reach great heights of achievement. Red surges upward and onward to victory, and denotes self-accomplishment. Human beings function efficiently when they march up the road, guided by Red's energy, toward the attainment of a goal. Seeking a goal gives purpose to life, and Red is a fountain of incentive which spurs man over obstacles and around barriers. With man's spirits so uplifted, chances of failure and disaster lessen.

Man is the only animal who can, if he chooses, sentence himself to a lifetime of drudgery. He may wear drab, uninteresting, lackluster colors and walk with his head lowered in imagined shame. Day after day, he builds a shell around himself until he finally sinks into the oblivion of "non-life." Red blasts this shell apart and ignites the fire of enthusiasm. Red projects a humming energy which is contagious to all who come in contact with it. This mighty color ignores self-pity and denial. Its watchword is "Why not!"

Don't be afraid to risk; don't be afraid to try! Enthusiasm will take you further than any amount of experience! Ralph Waldo Emerson wrote that "Nothing great was ever achieved without enthusiasm." Enthusiasm works like a tonic on boring jobs. Any task undertaken with enthusiasm is completed quickly, with far less disdain.

It takes courage to cast out the demons in your life, and Red color energy provides it. Confront those ghoulies who seek to slow you down, to foil your plans, or to sap you of enthusiasm. The Thwart Monster despises Red!

Red influences us in many ways we never thought about before. What is the significance of a "Red-letter day"? It's a cause for celebration! Waving a Red flag in front of a bull elicits immediate action! Anger is a healthy emotion, an emotion which is necessary to mental well-being. When we "see Red" and experience anger, an explosive blast of energy must be expelled in order to get on with feeling good. Sometimes a spurt of rich Red anger is just the thing to get us off the dime and out of a rut. Red makes things happen!

Secondarily, Red is protective, and it emboldens us to confront problems and defend our principles. In this context, Red prevents us from making the same mistakes again. We learn from misfortune, and Red color energy reminds us that we can avoid misery. The very best way to deal with making a mistake is the simplest: Simply say, "Oops! Made a mistake here!" and then go on! Mistakes never finish us; mistakes demonstrate knowledge. When we make an error, we can use that knowledge again, and apply it throughout life.

We will all be moody now and again, when we feel down and tired and oh-so-pitiful. But the solid truth is that melancholy is an emotion difficult to sustain. Red spurs us through melancholy and gets us going again.

One of the primary uses of Red color energy is for depression. Red involves the will to live and to live with passion. When feelings of inertia, fatigue, and sorrow—mental, physical, emotional, and spiritual—manifest themselves in your life, surround yourself in Red. Depression is rampant today and is characterized by a waning of feeling, an indifference to life. Eventually, unless aggressive, immediate steps are taken, depression leads to complete numbness of emotion. Red is a powerful weapon for battling depression. It jolts you out of depression and back into the teeming energy of life.

The raw power of Red is related to aggressiveness and conquest; it pushes us to be pioneers, to initiate action, and to lead a crusade forward. Red incites, and like the Little Red Choo-Choo, this glorious color yells out loud: I THINK I CAN, I THINK I CAN, I KNOW I CAN!

The warming qualities of Red make it an excellent remedy for chills and colds in that it seems to speed up blood circulation. Avoid using Red in the bedroom, for even though it intensifies passion, it also disturbs rest and relaxation. In study areas, Red is not good either, for this color calls out for movement and physical action. Game rooms and exercise areas look good done in Red.

Romantically, Red is a booster rocket. It leads a love relationship deeper in commitment and promise and provides that extra passion which intensifies joy. Red is the color of sexual excitement—it means blood and life in the urgency of procreation and intimacy. Throughout history, Red has been the color of sexual energy, as in Hawthorne's *The Scarlet Letter*. Red color energy represents seduction and the mutual rousing of passion. It sings a physical expression of devotion. The hallmark of Valentine's Day is the Red heart. Red denotes a great depth of passion in a love relationship. It is sexual in nature and very alluring: hot, vibrant Red accelerates emotional love into physical expression.

All comfortable relationships need a dollop of Red color

energy for a little excitement. While it is true that a marriage may lose some of its fire through the years, the flames of love can still burn brightly regardless of the passage of time. Red signals a desire for some enthusiastic response. Who wouldn't be moved by a pair of Red satin boxer shorts! A fire-engine Red slip peeking out from under an apron has got to evoke an immediate response! Passion has no age, and our powers to express ourselves sexually last a lifetime. But like anything else, if you don't use it, you lose it. Put some snap into a same-old relationship with a little alluring Red. Don't ignore that touch of wacky, silly, bubbly stuff inside you. That and a large dose of caring will ensure a lasting, satisfying love relationship. Do something right now with Red, and bring spontaneity and delight into your life!

Red is such a happy color!

□ *RICH ROSE* □

Rose is the higher octave of Red. It represents the gentler emotions such as compassion, sympathy, honor, and loyalty. These emotions are not less deep than those created by Red, but they possess a finer spiritual value. Rose also symbolizes self-love, forgiveness, sharing, sensitivity, and romance.

Rose color energy is spiritually revitalizing. It represents understanding and mercy. The milk of human kindness should justifiably be presented wrapped in Rose because it possesses a deep compassion for mankind and desires to help others. Compassion and sympathy are closely associated, and both are defined as the ability to feel empathy (to walk in someone else's moccasins) and to be supportive.

Rose is the color of good judgment: it recognizes respect, honor, and esteem. In this color, it is easy to accept the worth of a fellow—we see with a clear but loving eye and distinguish between what is real and what is not. Rose successfully arbitrates disputes. When we appreciate the moods or beliefs of others, relationships become compatible. Rose color energy heralds loyalty. Loyalty demonstrates dependability, reliability, and requires a certain strength of mind in order to stand fast beside an idea, a person, or a principle. Rose indicates a disgust of those who sway like reeds in the wind, those chameleons who turn the color of the rock they're on.

Honor is what you feel when you hold something or somebody in high esteem. It is a nobleness of mind, a shining, perfect thing sought after by those who seek goodness. The road to honor is paved by respect, and Rose carries the banner. Respect must be earned; it cannot be given to those who do not deserve it and it cannot be taken away at a whim. Admiration is not respect and neither is regard. To honor requires some activity on your part; it requires that you acknowledge it and praise it. Not to do so is moral embezzlement. Not to award merit for honorable behavior is cheap. High awards are sometimes given in the form of a Rosette.

Just as you honor and respect worthy others, you must feel the same for yourself. Self-love is as necessary as oxygen to the happy human being. If you do not love yourself, you condemn yourself to never being satisfied, never feeling complete, and always searching but never finding the elusive "self" that enables you to "be." Do not become blind to your own beauty. View that Rosy picture of yourself and identify your wonderful, unique qualities. When you can love yourself, accepting your own frailties and your own humanity, only then can you love another. Rose color energy is the symbol of the renewal of love, for self and for others. Through self-love you see life through Rose-colored glasses, and when you love yourself, you have nothing more to prove. Accept your shortcomings—this makes it easier to accept the shortcomings of others. Forgive yourself for not being perfect—to expect human perfection is ludicrous, because even the Father knows we are not perfect. We can, however, strive for perfection and hold a proper regard for our own capabilities.

The great men we admire today began as ordinary people, just like you. They possessed a vision and sought success (just like you); they blundered along, making mistakes (just like you), and they feared the unknown (just like you). But those great men we admire today possess the very same gifts that you possess right now.

Rose energy stands for forgiveness in all its forms: broken relationships, broken promises, broken bodies, careless words, and lies. All of these carry pain, and all were caused by someone's actions. These deeds are history and nothing can turn back time to make them not occur. So what is to be done? Acknowledge and forgive. Rose energy enables us to respond with love to a wrong done to us. The alternative to forgiveness is not a right that belongs to us . . . the alternative to forgiveness is vengeance. It is simply not in our power to make a vengeance judgment stick; that duty belongs to God. Gentle Rose eases the pain and gently urges us to forgive.

Rose is for sharing: the gift of a single Rose is a significant message of love indicating a reciprocal affection. It has been said that the ultimate sharing experience is a well-proportioned love that strikes an equitable balance. Remember that balance and harmony signify the ultimate in healthy life. To share means to enrich, both ourselves and others. The depth of love can be measured by the degree to which we are willing to share our lives with someone else. To share the most valuable, the most honorable part of ourselves is the epitome of blessed experiences—through this commingling we discover what it means when two become one.

Rose is also a disciplined administrator which turns dreams into realities. When channeled toward a goal, Rose expects that the path might be rocky, but it is determined to fight for right, honor, and truth. This energy depicts sensitivity in the workplace. We spend a vast amount of time working with others, and it is necessary that we make this time pleasant and productive. Rose color energy opens the channel of acceptance and respect from coworkers. It speaks out calmly but distinctly: it states that a worker should do his job to the best of his ability, demonstrate dependability and a cooperative manner, and is therefore deserving of respect. Rose in the workplace promotes effective communications, the meshing of varied personalities, and efficiency.

If romance is the music of the heart, Rose is its melody. Exalted love, virtue, and devotion are hallmarks of this sweet color. It is the cream which rises to the top, and its rich, comforting texture brings ease to hurt feelings. Love is the greatest need of all human needs, and none of us can survive without it. Rose personifies unselfish, true love. Symbolizing constant affection, Rose enhances sweet romance. It is aware of the emotional state of others. Rose emits tender, gentle rays and cocoons the delicate flower of romance in warm feelings. It takes so little effort to open our arms to another, and Rose energy allows us to connect. This beautiful color is love energy in action. Rose nurtures, cares for, accepts, adores. It is the fine mist of fantasy and the exalted virtues of love. Rose is the beginning of deep, abiding true love. Romance is not lust or sex or companionship or obsession or transitory interest. Rose energy depicts romance in all its glory and shows us the way to real love. It realizes romantic dreams and enlightens the path to making those dreams come true. The Rose vibration calls out to love, and like a magnet, it draws romance into our lives.

□ *TRUE ORANGE* □

This bright color is a social energy. Orange bounces around with a feeling of great well-being; it unites and cooperates.

Orange handles fear, insecurity, remorse, guilt, loneliness, prejudice, and bad habits. This energy works to heal ailments of the respiratory system. It is the energy for change and the color of hope.

When the need arises to bring people, information, and circumstances into sync, Orange color energy should be present. It helps all parties to see all sides of a situation and uses tact and diplomacy to reach compromises. Orange aids a smoothly functioning team by fostering a deeper interest in and concern for coworkers. A collaborative effort is sometimes the hardest result to achieve because there is such a diversity of ideas, people, and priorities. Orange provides an atmosphere of noncompetitive rapport.

Along these lines, when a unified effort is required at work or at home, Orange energy oils the wheels of effort. It brings people together in harmony. Harmony is that blessed state of existence when all members work as one, when all strive for a common goal, and when priorities are aligned together. An immense amount of energy can be expended, purposelessly, when coworkers squabble among themselves. In a family situation, the same is true: squabbling never accomplishes any goal, it only creates irritable personalities who fume and fuss and leave the goal ignored.

Orange is mellow, laid-back. Emotionally, these rays enhance self-confidence and banish timidity. The A. A. Milne character Tigger is a wonderful example of exuberant Orange. Friendly and approachable, Orange emits a welcoming energy and calls human beings together for contented fellowship. This joyous color fosters a feeling of service and concern for the welfare of all. A person dressed in bright Orange is hard to resist.

Fear is agitation or dismay in the anticipation of or in the presence of danger. Don't ignore fear because it is a signal of danger, but view fear as just that: a signal. When your entire life is governed by fear, you set out to sabotage your own happiness. If actions are determined by fear of failure, fear of superiors, fear of embarrassment, fear of pain, or any other fear, our lives cannot be lived happily. We spend our time and energy avoiding imagined and fearful results, so we are always moving laterally or backward, and we never move forward. We never accomplish anything because we are too busy avoiding something we fear. Orange is a warm, upbeat ray, and it can help deal with fear.

A bonus that Orange color energy provides is its help in overcoming bad habits. Surprisingly, this positive color helps us follow good rules and eschew bad practices. The following list of yukky things are only bad habits: prejudice, loneliness, insecurity, remorse, and guilt.

Yes, they are only bad habits. Bad habits signal that the Thwart Monster is at work. He loves repetitive, destructive behaviors. You can teach yourself to break bad habits, and Orange energy helps.

Prejudice is an opinion formed without taking time and care to judge fairly. Work away from feeling prejudiced against others or yourself. Orange overcomes unfair bias. It just can't abide disharmony among human beings. When countries meet to discuss problems, Orange color energy should surround the entire group! This would be ideal since Orange is a mixture of vital Red and intellectual Yellow.

Loneliness and aloneness are two different dogs. Some solitary time is healing and positive, but loneliness is a desperate state of mind. It is very simple to overcome loneliness, so listen carefully: if you develop a love for yourself, if you feel comfortable being you, alone, then others will naturally gravitate toward you. They will want to be around someone who emits such positive vibrations, someone who projects such a positive self-image. To promote a feeling of well-being in self, use Orange and its magnetizing rays to do away with loneliness and cultivate appropriate aloneness.

Orange energy rays simply float away insecurities. Insecurity is not a feeling; it is a judgment we pass on ourselves. So what if you are not a rocket scientist? Maybe that rocket scientist can't balance his checkbook. And so what if you flunked sophomore algebra; maybe that math whiz can't bait a hook. So don't be so hard on yourself. Glory in another's ability, but don't fail to glory in your own, unique abilities.

Orange is useful in dealing with guilt, the most crippling emotion of mankind. Human beings are extremely presumptuous when they choose to feel guilty. Guilt is something which will or will not be assigned by the Father, not by us. While we may regret certain actions or wrongdoings, and while we may feel remorseful or penitent about what we've done or said, it is our responsibility to apologize and get over it. If we dwell on nasty guilt, we allow it to become monstrously out of proportion. We can never get even with ourselves unless we choose to lay it down and go on. When you come to terms with past guilt, Orange is there to instill a positive new beginning. Orange rockets us into the exciting future, where we confidently make wise decisions and stride off in new directions.

Orange knocks out fear of change and allows us to courageously face the unknown. We were put on earth to grow and learn, and adaptability to change is the means we use to get from one plane to another. Change is exciting; it offers opportunities galore. When we are afraid to change, we are afraid to feel better, look better, perform better, and know more. Don't be afraid of change—embrace it! Orange carries the vanguard of cheerful, positive changes.

Most important, Orange is the color of hope. There is no elixir so life-giving, no tonic so vital as hope. Of our many blessings, hope is the greatest, for hope makes the hard times of life bearable and provides a fountain of incentive for the spirit. Hope heals, and Orange is a dynamic healing energy. Sometimes, in the midst of a crisis, hope is the only thing we can cling to in order to get through it. Hope is a balm to the spirit, and Orange, with its warmth and welcome, soothes anxiety and promotes positive, life-giving hope. When the eyes light upon a splash of Orange, it is just like getting a second wind. We are inspired to move onward, to try again, to keep pumping.

And, since Orange is such a heavy-duty, healing energy, it works well for asthma, bronchitis, coughs, and other ailments of the lungs. In this regard, Orange color energy is a respiratory stimulant. As a matter of fact, Orange stimulates the entire physical makeup.

Use Orange in areas where groups of people congregate. It enhances the positive flow of energy between persons and encourages timid ones to contribute in a positive way. A splash of Orange in areas where people collaborate makes the atmosphere noncompetitive and compatible. When human beings deal reasonably with one another, barriers can be destroyed and mountains moved.

□ *GLISTENING GOLD* □

Congenial like Orange, Gold possesses a higher level of spiritual happiness, attainment, and wisdom. It represents the beauty of life and the soul. Gold energy provides encouragement, tolerance, comfort, warmth, and openness.

Gold is the wise one, the teacher, and its purpose is communication. It does not seek to dominate or overwhelm, but it opens the door to the sharing of feelings and the interchange of ideas. Through discussion, people gain insight and knowledge from one another. With Gold rays surrounding you, unobstructed communication is possible, and people become candid with each other. Gold suggests and advises.

With a deep feeling for mankind, Gold comforts those in conflict and grants tolerance. Gold makes no value judgments and gives no definite directions for action; it simply allows people to find wisdom in its radiant light.

Gold energy cheers and gladdens the heart. This is the color of happiness and laughter: it is friendly, warmhearted, and compassionate. It gives life grace and depth. Correspondent to the energies of Orange, Gold is the light of joy—it radiates happiness—and in its light, everyone feels like having fun!

This higher octave of Orange possesses great energy, but channels its force into spiritual awakening. It promotes a profound feeling of the beauty of life and life's possibilities for success. With Gold we identify the radiant glory of the sun, whose name comes from *sol,* or soul.

Gold encourages us to a spiritual rebirth; its rays give us a boost and urge us onward toward success. Gold is reassuring, and in its rays we are strengthened and supported.

□ *DAFFODIL YELLOW* □

Holding first place in the spectrum for maximum brightness and luminosity, Yellow spreads sunshine—it is the color of intellectual illumination, creativity, the synthesis of new ideas, and optimism. Yellow is physically health-giving and healing, and its use helps alleviate certain emotional problems.

The portions of the mind concerned with reasoning, analysis, and integration of ideas into practical life are stimulated by this positive magnetic vibration. In Yellow's glow, the innovative juices flow and we are urged to take on challenges and explore new directions. In this light we find ourselves adaptable to change, flexible in rerouting life's direction. Fear of change is somehow blown away with this ray, and imaginative new ideas and thoughts spring unsummoned into the mind. This is particularly important as it relates to career and job. We can be assertive (but not obnoxious), imaginative without being unrealistic, and assured but not pushy.

Yellow's stimulation of the mental faculties is very important because this is where the command center of deductive reasoning is located. The mind must follow certain logical thought processes in order to make decisions, put together plans, set goals, and reason through problems. Yellow energy also stimulates human beings in a spiritual way. We are better able to understand and clarify the mysterious powers of the mind.

Yellow allows human beings to exercise that sometimes dormant ability, creativity, to its fullest capacity. Creative visualizations are clarified and sharpened with the use of Yellow vibrations. We can see, in infinite detail, desired mind pictures we want manifested in our lives.

Illumined in vibrant Yellow rays, the mind seeks creative outlets; the self is expressed through different and often innovative methods. We can apply abstract solutions to concrete problems, often with great results!

This lively color allows us to synthesize our new creative ideas. It gives us the ability to put parts together to form a whole, which is a form of deductive reasoning. Correct solutions to problems, remission of negative feelings, intensified ambition, and ways to see ambition achieved are easily found with Yellow.

Yellow stimulates the absorption reflex of the mind. We can train the mind to function like a sponge in absorbing information. Spurred on by this positive energy, the mind quickly and accurately fits this information together like pieces of a puzzle. All becomes clear in Yellow's glow.

Yellow is the optimist; it always looks for the positive characteristics of any person or situation. The optimist is constantly refreshed mentally. To obtain or deepen a real zest for life, Yellow shows the way. The optimist revels in learning and creating through objective measures and makes good subjective judgments along the way.

Certain negative personality traits can be dealt with constructively and sometimes alleviated with Yellow! This buttery-colored energy diminishes jealousy, shame, disgrace, and dishonor.

Sufferers of low self-esteem have difficulty with self-expression. Yellow offers a little boldness in the expression of self, and elevates the one who wallows in pity.

Yellow is greatly beneficial in physical ways; it aids in good digestion. Ever heard of nervous stomach? It can cause all kinds of minor physical ailments. Yellow energy seems to ease strung-out, tightened-up nerves. Consequently, illnesses caused by "nerves" can be helped or healed entirely. Everyone needs some method to release tension, and Yellow uncramps muscles and relaxes the body. Good for mental exhaustion, a Yellow light-bath provides inspiration; it awakens the joy in us and minimizes chaotic thought patterns. When you feel an attack of nerves coming on, pick a buttercup and contemplate its beauty and color; this little Yellow flower reminds us that we can always feel young-at-heart. Place problems on the back burner and pick up some fairy dust on the end of your nose. This buttercup therapy is very beneficial.

A bonus is Yellow's effect on the skin: it opens pores and helps the body rid itself of nervous sweat or fear perspiration. Have you heard the expression "animals can smell fear"? This adage is rooted in fact. Have you ever drowsed on the porch in the warm sun? Our poor, battered bodies just relax and melt in caressing Yellow sunlight.

A decor centered around Yellow tones is successful in rooms where stimulated mental activity is desired, like libraries, study rooms, and business think tanks. Whenever you need an answer to a difficult problem, surround yourself with Yellow and find solutions easily without stress. If a difficult concept or plan needs to be presented quickly and effectively, Yellow aids the speaker and the audience to grasp all the important parts of the matter.

□ *GLORIOUS GREEN* □

Separating the stimulating colors from the calming colors, Green occupies the center of the spectrum. It represents balance, and as such it symbolizes the alignment of life's material aspects with the spiritual side of man. Green is a passive color, but possesses a magnetic appeal which normalizes and orders all forces of the universe. This energy successfully harmonizes the thermal (heat) colors of the spectrum and the electric (cool) colors on the opposite end of the spectrum.

The color of nature affects the commingling of soul with spirit, harmony, the life force, healing, self-regulation, purpose, awareness, and prosperity.

With balance as its watchword, Green promotes the maturation of man's physical body with his spiritual self. When these two aspects are aligned, the greatest constructive power of the universe is active. Man is complete in the Green rays: his spiritual self is balanced with his material or tangible being. Our heads may be in spiritual clouds, but our feet remain planted firmly on the ground. Green is the color of wholeness.

Life, with all its glorious productivity and growth, is represented in the Green rays. Rejuvenation and stimulation of growth and health are alive in this energy. Green color energy predominates in nature, the environment created by the Father. All of nature adorns herself in robes of lush Greenery to emit powerful and magnetic life forces.

It is reasonable also that Green is a strong healing ray. Nature's environment teems with life. Green is a signpost of natural health. With its fresh, soothing emanations, life explodes and expands into beauty under Green's rays. At rest, the body rejuvenates itself—nature gathers power to grow and create new life.

Green has an astringent quality which alleviates strain through balancing. This energy helps soothe tension in muscles and nerves. It relaxes the nervous system and induces calmness. It is within this calm state that Green's antiseptic qualities aid in destroying bacteria and preventing decay in the body. Green is the energy for all ailments of the heart: blood pressure, hypertension, hyperactivity, heart diseases, stomach ulcers (which stress the heart), nonspecific aches and pains, and muscle spasms. In short, the body responds to Green energy in the realm of tension control; it eases emotional states which cause physical illnesses.

Green also heals emotional wounds. In its sheltering light, we feel safe to turn loose our pent-up emotions. A hot, writhing mass of bad feelings does nothing to promote good health. But when we are balanced, these negative influences flow out of the body, mind, and spirit and are replaced by calm strength. Sometimes negative emotions manifest themselves in a surge of undirected energy. Human beings are built for work, and work is a good outlet for this energy. Secondarily, the satisfaction of a job well and completely done makes man proud and happy with himself.

Green symbolizes self-regulation and the path to self-awareness. It personifies the establishment of order and consistency in life. This energy allows us to enforce necessary and healthful routines in our lives and recognize the importance of precision and efficiency. Green seeks to support the solid foundations of man's principles and allows us to give shape to our ideas and dreams. We are able to complete tasks, identify results, and give form to intangible ideas. Our durable bodies expand with good health and excel at turning thoughts into reality. Green clarifies the purpose of life; it is stabilizing and steadfast.

Finding a purpose in life is blocked many times, so when a feeling of befuddlement invades the temperament, use Green color energy to clarify your purpose. Human beings are useless without a purpose. There it is. Straight out. If you drift along throughout the minutes, seconds, and hours of your life, holding no standard true and real, striving for no concrete goal, tossed about on every whim of acquaintances, your life has no basic meaning. And doesn't the Father give us great and wonderful gifts of talent and ability? Isn't it our purpose in life to develop those gifts?

In a peaceful, serene environment provided by the Green ray, static forces are neutralized with Divine Power. When His children are aligned with Him spiritually, the Father blesses us with a lack of disorder and an abundance of good health, competence, and production. All organizational skills and all management rules and efficiency have their foundation in Green.

And of course Green is the money color. This ray promotes prosperity, growth, and renewal. Powerful and magnetic life emanations shine from Green, and this force attracts abundance and wealth. Good fortune fairly oozes from Green surroundings. The fertile earth yields incredible wealth, and this wealth is available to earth's inhabitants. Wealth, however, does not just fall into a bank account. It must be worked for, sometimes very hard. Since Green provides balance, and balance is the ideal goal of life, realize that balance means lack of poverty and the promise of economic stability. Concentrate on Green's prosperous power in a shaky financial situation.

Human beings have the power to sentence themselves

to a life of purposeless wandering and poverty. We can wallow and thrash around, wrestling with the Without Syndrome, never resting well or enjoying good health. Or we can light a Green candle, gaze at lush Green vegetation, surround ourselves with this pulsing life force, and commit ourselves to growth and health.

□ *COOL BLUE* □

As we move toward the Blue-Indigo-Violet-Purple end of the spectrum, and away from the Red-Yellow-Orange, the energy becomes finer and cooler. Blue, the first color of this division, represents a serene, less physically stimulating, more astringent vibration.

Blue is traditionally the color of spirit. It symbolizes understanding and spiritual development, inner happiness, the will (man's and the Higher Spirit's), religiosity, faith, patience, safe travel, dealing with grief and loss, and tranquillity.

The color of the sky and the sea inspires a vision of infinity, combining human and spiritual aspects of life. Blue gives a feeling of depth and lifts man from concerns of the body upward to the realm of higher consciousness and spiritual inspiration. It appears clear that man is raised above the coarse vibrations of material concerns in the Blue rays; this color makes the first steps toward becoming a spiritual person easy to take. Blue prompts the mind to evolve the self-concept. Consider the vastness of the sky and sea—this vision allows us to transcend pettiness and sets us upon an introspective journey.

When the spirit of man is at peace, on a sea of tranquil Blue, his inner happiness and wholeness are attainable. This inner happiness is not just a lack of worry or anxiety—just as joy is not simply the absence of pain—but if man desires his inner serenity, he must begin to flood himself and his immediate environment with Blue rays. Through the use of this energy, self-understanding unfolds.

It is man's basic responsibility to take the bountiful gifts from the Father and to develop them, thereby evolving into a higher being. With Blue emanations we are ignited by spiritual fire. We are illumined to strive for perfection. Do not curse fate or others for the current circumstances of your life, but recognize that you alone are responsible for those circumstances, and you are responsible for changing them. Happiness is our human birthright, and it is our highest moral imperative to achieve it. You cannot lift yourself up by suffering. You must put aside suffering, which is passivity, self-pity, or giving up. Make yourself happy by achievement, attainment of goals, and living according to your own moral standards. This is an explanation of "will."

Man's will, throughout the mental, physical, and emotional body, is the fuel by which we move toward enlightenment. When man's will is aligned with the Father's Will, no obstacle is too great to overcome. Bathed in Blue light we can achieve the union of our will with the Father's Will. We leave the restless, sensory-stimulated, earthly will behind and nurture inner sensitivity; we foster our natural yearning for oneness with a Higher Power.

Blue deepens faith; it renews faith. Blue represents contentment, understanding, and a surety—an inner knowing—that man possesses the basic tools of success inside himself. And that success is possible. Happiness is a Divine Right, and faith is the path to obtain it. Many people who concentrate on faith to guide their lives are religious.

More practically, Blue soothes worries and grants patience. We are tolerant and composed in its energy.

Immersed in Blue energy, the mind, body, and spirit become calm, so it naturally follows that grief is lessened and loss becomes bearable. Calling upon Blue's sustaining, faithful rays, man is better able to adjust after the death of a loved one or some other great loss. Blue soothes all kinds and types of anxiety. One woman wore a small Blue ribbon pinned to her blouse when she endured an IRS audit. She professed that in any situation in which she was worried, anxious, nervous, or just plain scared, the little Blue ribbon pinned to her blouse reminded her of spiritual blessings and strength. Human beings need a little extra energy in a crisis, a little dose of tranquillity. These days, if everyone who was stressed or worried wore Blue, we'd be awash like the ocean in this beautiful color!

Blue accents or background colors are excellent in the bedroom: Blue helps the poor insomniac. It possesses a tranquil vibration and calms the mind, which leads to peaceful sleep. And sleep is nature's medicine for the body. Blue is helpful for headaches or any malady associated with the head area.

Blue is the perfect environment in which to reflect on spiritual values. These vibrations energize a devotional power, bringing up the ability to recognize spiritual qualities. Through Blue color energy, human beings rise above the meaningless scramble of earthly life and unfold like flowers into spiritual maturity. We are safeguarded on this journey by Blue color energy; in fact, use Blue to ensure safe travel on any kind of journey.

☐ *DEEP INDIGO* ☐

This deep, rich color is a combination of Violet and Blue. Indigo is the color of the dye used to color jeans. It is smoothly textured and lustrous. Moving further into the spiritual realm of life, Indigo symbolizes man's spiritual eye. In this ray is found introspection, self-contemplation and analysis, self-discipline, increased intuitive powers, skills to overcome worry and anxiety, justice, memory, forgiving in romantic love, and family unity and environment.

In the light of this spiritual ray, man is able to contemplate his "self." Indigo aids the seeker in examining and analyzing his thoughts and feelings. Man may reflect on his talents, abilities, and emotional strengths, and develop a deep spiritual understanding of himself. Those who are not afraid to delve into the murky waters of the self might find themselves regenerated in Indigo's energy. New fields of comprehension and self-knowledge might become clear. Inner vision could be extended, which will expand the consciousness of the universe. Indigo helps man to more clearly perceive the reality of the life process; the spiritual eye sees beyond physical manifestations. In this ray, our many-faceted natures—mental, physical, emotional, spiritual—become more fully integrated and understood.

Along the path to enlightenment, we are able to answer great philosophical questions . . . at least as they apply to ourselves. The abstract fuses with the concrete, the tangible with the intangible. We strive toward wholeness, and in Indigo's light, this is more easily achieved.

It follows naturally with this introspection that our intuitive powers increase. We are more receptive to hunches and instinctive feelings. Man's sixth sense has not been fully developed yet and it lies still within the realm of phenomena. With the help of caressing Indigo rays, perception spontaneously awakens. Intuitive powers beckon us to explore other stages of consciousness and other levels of spiritual enlightenment. Indigo is a color worn often by meditative teachers and students.

Indigo's intuitive faculty encourages fears, frustrations, and worries to float away from the body, then it seals the aura and forbids negative energy from seeping in. There is no room for negative energy within the whole, healthy mind. Indigo also works to lessen stress, which is a nonspecific bodily response to some outside stimulus; each person reacts differently to stress. Stress causes all kinds of human problems, but it finds difficulty in getting around Indigo's protective shield.

Indigo is the color of justice. As a moral principle, justice is necessary even unto survival. In its rays, man is able to reconcile problems fairly. In Indigo's light, man recognizes his true character. He must judge himself with incorruptible vision, and value others accordingly. He must cleave to an honorable existence. If he treats others with justice, he is entitled to justice in return, which is all any of us deserve.

Human beings lack self-discipline. Some of our habits are destructive: our thoughts are chaotic and we are unable to manage our money, time, or energy successfully. Success and happiness require a tremendous amount of self-discipline, and in Indigo's spiritually supportive rays, self-discipline is more fully developed.

Ever had problems with a bad memory? Treat this malady with Indigo. Forgetfulness is frustrating—also embarrassing. We feel vulnerable when we cannot remember. It is said that the memory is not a videotape, but the mind is a wonderful camera. If you control the process of memory, fantastically detailed data are available to you. If you have a poor memory, there is a wealth of information and practice programs to aid you. Study this problem bathed in Indigo light.

Indigo is the peacemaker. Its emblem is universality and its function is fairness. Human beings will have differences, but with Indigo's help, problems are resolved and harmony reigns. This is especially true for the family. As the color of the family peacemaker, Indigo fosters acceptance and tolerance, encourages compromise, and reveals that strength in love will carry the family unit through any hard time. Indigo lessens panic. Anxiety is inner conflict, and it may take on many different forms. Indigo aids inner conflict too.

Romantically, Indigo helps develop a forgiving nature. Part of a partnership or marriage or permanent arrangement between lovers is the art of forgiving. When we choose to share our lives with another, we must be prepared to overlook occasional insensitivity. Sometimes, this type of behavior is truly accidental, and when it is, we must be prepared to forgive and go on. That is not to say that we must be prepared to tolerate such behaviors all the time, but if we look closely at ourselves, honestly, we'll discover that at times we too have been thoughtless and inconsiderate. Indigo's open mind and forgiving nature allow love to grow, for no human love is without its faults.

Indigo's energy permits the growth of true love by granting freedom to the partners. As individuals, freedom to change and grow, risk and triumph, is necessary to the maturing process. Love must also remain free, and lovers need to practice constructive open-mindedness; lovers should encourage one another to feel free to adapt, change, and grow. Recognizing that sometimes one lover will get his way and vice versa promotes the deepening of the love relationship.

□ *CLEAR VIOLET* □

Violet, which includes royal Purple, is the highest color vibration of the spectrum and therefore has the shortest wavelength. It is a blend of Red and Blue, and is the most spiritual of colors. It is the energy of self-transformation.

Violet represents confidence and dignity, overcoming self-pity, gossip and other barriers to happiness, personal attainment, form and ceremony, and spiritual maturity.

Dignity describes self-confidence in action. As human beings awaken to their unique capabilities, Violet completes the bonding of reality with spirituality. If man is confident in who he is and his purpose, and believes in his ability to achieve his purpose, he demonstrates a high sense of personal integrity and is consequently very attractive to others. His bearing and carriage send a message of personal dignity. He demands complete honesty from others and is not blown like a wisp on the winds of pure emotion. Violet symbolizes idealism and the acting-out of honor in everyday life. The person who acts as he believes is one step from complete spirituality: the alignment of the person with the Father. Self-confidence makes self-dignity possible.

This shimmering color strives to understand and work with the reality of the life process. In its rays we find great influences: consideration, universal consciousness, positivity, nobility, and knowledge. Violet directs from the spirit to the physical.

Possessing the devotion of Blue and the intuition of Indigo, Violet is concerned with the most advanced phases of spiritual development. It probes the depths of any situation, looking beyond the surface, and asks why.

Violet loves form and ceremony. Most stained-glass windows in churches or other places of spiritual essence use Violet or Purple to depict holy events. Kings and other royal figures are "born to the Purple." Priests' vestments are beautifully embroidered and decorated with this color. A predominantly Violet environment creates an inspiring atmosphere. Some people associate Violet with sorrow, but it does not imply sadness—this energy simply makes us spiritually mindful and reverent.

Because of its supreme state of consciousness, Violet enables us to overcome man-made obstacles. This ray banishes evil influences; this energy rises above earthly barriers. Spotless ethics, unqualified merit, and nobility describe Violet's effect. Problems cannot move this energy: it simply does not acknowledge that evil attempts to triumph. Sometimes, though, it is good to realize that obstacles are opportunities and provide us with those awful "learning experiences." Use Violet to transcend earthly barriers.

Violet's finely vibrating energy is a strong medicine for self-pity and gossipers. These rays simply do not participate in self-pity and will not tolerate gossip, lies, and shameful behavior of this sort. This energy helps us overcome self-pity and the poor-me mind-set.

Most of all, Violet represents spiritual maturity. As you can see, if one remains faithful, overcomes obstacles, rises nobly to an occasion, and cherishes Oneness with the Father, he approaches spiritual maturity. The rapture enjoyed by those who achieve this plane is incredible.

Violet is the fine energy which uplifts the consciousness toward personal spiritual attainment. The genuine essence of life can be seen reflected in Violet rays of light. This color energy is tireless when it comes to enlightenment or spiritual awakening. It is not preoccupied with worldly sensations; it seeks instead to illumine man's purpose, his faith and perception, and the essential security of man's inner self. Violet sends man on perfection's path. Man finds that he is a spiritual being and that perfect happiness is realized through alignment with the Creative Source, the Father.

□ *RADIANT WHITE* □

White is the ultimate expression of Oneness with the Father, blessings in the home, fidelity, sincerity, pure faith, overcoming temptations, honesty, purity, and mercy.

White is the essence of all colors, containing all aspects of every color. White color energy demonstrates the active manifestation of all that is perfect in life. As the highest concept of man, White enables him to attain perfection.

For when man is united with the Father, absolute harmony exists and a state of perfect enlightenment is achieved.

Within purifying White rays, we discover the totality of our being and purpose. We reach the zenith of goodness and wisdom: all is made clear, all is explained, all is understood, all is accomplished. Enlightenment is that state when human beings accept spiritual knowledge intellectually and then apply it in a practical manner. In pure White light, inadequacies vanish, fears fade away, superstition and ignorance disintegrate.

When man is one with the Father, he is filled with radiant energy and superhuman powers. He is transformed from commonality into blessedness. There is no wrongness, no unbalanced feelings, no fear. In White's energy, there is room for no other standards but truth, honor, fidelity, and integrity. Man is shown at his highest spirituality.

The soul's armor is White light; it protects and cleanses. It repels all attacks on man's goodness, and in so doing, it drives fear from within our minds. White makes us immune to depravity, violence, and dread. Use White to heal all illnesses and all wounds. Use White as a reminder of our own special blessedness.

White color energy depicts fidelity. It aids us in being true to others and true to ourselves. As a stabilizing influence, this ray enables committed partners to hold their relationship above pettiness. It makes us unafraid to promise and unafraid to follow through on our vows. Fidelity is desperately needed by human beings today. The universe is filled with the wails of many, crying out for others who are true. It is not difficult to be faithful; it is a precious jewel in the crown of the love relationship. Betrayal slashes deep wounds into the most vulnerable part of the human heart. If a love relationship has ended, then it must end, and betrayal before the end of one relationship and the beginning of another is tragic. The pain spawned by such behavior takes years to deal with and overcome. The person who will not let go of one partner unless there is another waiting in the wings is much to be pitied. This practice is a sad reflection of the person's self-image. White's spiritual energy is inexhaustible toward the goal of fidelity.

If you want to overcome temptation, saturate yourself in White. If you are experiencing moral doubts about something, contemplate the situation surrounded by White. The perfect solution to any difficulty is illumined in White's color energy.

Since time began, Wise men or Illuminati have used White to signify the highest quality of life. They believed that this energy contained the active manifestation of all life—its very essence and perfection. Representing not only the spiritual enlightenment of the soul, White suggests that physical man may tune in to the higher levels of consciousness. This rare and pure vibration represents positive, cleansing energy which is an infallible shield against all that is evil in the universe.

All that is good and pure in life is usually depicted in White: nurses, health care professionals (they wear White when it would seem more reasonable to wear something that does not show spots), brides, religious leaders and participants, and those who yearn for perfection or seek a holy vision.

White light is pure love, kindness, goodness, fulfillment, and awakening. Its energy refreshes and rekindles and manifests a positive power that shakes the pillars of heaven. White is the flag of the celestial odyssey and the holy quest; it is the beginning and the end; it is an energy which allows man's inner exploration and advancement to wisdom. White is the light of the Master.

□ *THE WHITE LIGHT OF SPIRIT* □

The White Light of Spirit is the combination of all energy rays, all wisdom, and the realization of man's Oneness with the Father or man rising to his full potential. Since the color White is the combination of all color rays, it contains every energy in the universe. It is the perfect blending of the material plane and the intangible spiritual plane and grants perfect balance and harmony. The White Light of Spirit is powered by complete love: the Father for man, and mankind for his Divine Source or Creator.

Human beings cannot "see" this light, but it warms us and illumines us. Its home is the sanctuary of the soul. If the body is a holy temple, the radiant center of the temple is the White Light of Spirit. Man calls upon this energy, spark by spark, to move through his days. The White Light banishes the Thwart Monster—he cannot abide this pure energy—and it cures the Without Syndrome, for when man is illumined by the White Light of his Spirit, no lack, no want, no sorrow can exist.

Contained in your White Light of Spirit within is all the true knowledge about that unique being which is yourself. It also contains understandable information about the Father. He (for consistency's sake we use this pronoun) is a benevolent, loving God, full of immeasurable power and glory. He wants us to come close and be protected; He wants us to call upon the storehouse of power He has created within us to achieve great things.

As many people as there are in the universe, that is the number of descriptions for the Father. Each man beholds Him differently. There is no truer friend, no more passionate supporter, no more affirmative source of power than the Father. Get to know your Divine Source, Higher Consciousness, Christ Self, or any other name for your Creator. With this knowing all is possible, all is achieved.

□ *TAKING CONTROL OF LIFE AND LETTING GO OF PROBLEMS* □

Man has the potential to become a heroic being. He was endowed with every characteristic, trait, and power needed to earn the title of hero. All of man's power comes from the Father, carried straight as an arrow from Him to the mind of man. When our bodies, minds, and spirits are aligned (in harmony with the Father), all that energy is concentrated and focused. It springs eternal from inside us to be used for whatever we need.

What we must do is take control of this power. *We* are in charge of it; *we* control. *We* focus our energy, and it is the fuel we use to drive ourselves to higher consciousness and higher achievement. Do you now understand how great this energy is? Do you now realize that it is the greatest tool of all? It makes perfect, reasonable sense to use color energy along with the spoken word to be happy—how foolish we have been to take color and the spoken word for granted, ignoring their power and allowing the wise use of these energies to languish unused while we scramble for a get-rich-quick scheme or a miracle drug or a magic wand.

Use your personal power to let go of problems and petty worries. It is a crime to use your power for jealousy, manipulative games, negative feelings, and evil intents. Turn instead to the affirmative, positive trail. Use your precious energy to love, and laugh, and create happiness. Use it to acquire knowledge and skill, to understand yourself, others, and the intricate design of life. All the power you will ever need radiates from inside you, and it is your responsibility to use it for good, for it is our belief that man will ultimately be judged on what he has accomplished in his allotted time.

How foolish and wasteful to hang on to regrets and

guilt from the past. How blind we are when we complain, hold grudges, deny forgiveness, and wallow around in old sorrows. Is it not true that a negative activity like picking the scab of an old wound achieves nothing but pain? And is it not true that self-actualization brings a feeling of accomplishment . . . for even if we do not have resounding success in a chosen task, we at least have given it our best effort? Life is not ordinary. It is not a series of problems, blocks, and obstacles. It is a series of opportunities, miracles, and happy occasions. Henry Ford said, "Think you can, think you can't, either way you're right."

Begin now to move forward on the journey to enlightenment. The greatest crime of all is to remain wedded to a past triumph or disaster, and we will surely find what we seek, be it future triumphs or future disasters. The greatest crime is not to grow.

□ *INTUITION* □

We receive knowledge, information, and cues from our own intuition. Hunches, the sixth sense, gut reactions, sneaky feelings, déjà vu, and a hundred other words describe this indescribable happening called intuition. If we make ourselves into a clear and perfect open channel to the Father, a wealth of information showers upon us: guidance and direction, plans of action, warnings and encouragements come through loud and clear.

When we ignore intuition, we turn loose of the lifeline which binds us to the Father. Don't ever ignore your intuition. Intuition is a spiritual faculty which points the way; it is a compass which keeps us on course. Listening closely to and acting upon the intuition lays the foundation of our lives for . . .

□ *MIRACLES!* □

It is man's divine right to have everything he needs, and more. Plenty, even. When human beings depend upon the gifts the Father has given us for total sustenance, the supply is inexhaustible. Faith and a strong belief are required. Active faith and unfailing belief in one's personal power and supply must be demonstrated. One must prepare for miracles.

To prepare, a person must expect what he wants (according to the Father's will for the good of all concerned) at the deepest levels of his being. He must prepare and get ready to receive it, and to proceed as if there was never any doubt about getting it.

A miracle is not a gift in the way we know the meaning of the word. While it is true that a gift is sometimes expected, spiritual gifts in the form of miracles can be depended upon to happen. The Father wants His children to be happy and fulfilled. When His children are one with Him, the Kingdom is theirs, already available, ready to be accepted.

It is not the Father's Will to make us do what we hate or receive what we cannot use and do not want. If we have those negative situations in our lives, it is because those negative situations are *man-made* not God-made. The Father wants us to rise above ordinary concerns and meet the world with joy and anticipation, knowing that all is well and only bounteous good is in store for us. This wonderful concept comes with a few strings, however.

We must be ready to accept our abundance, and when we do we must use it to the best advantage to accomplish the most good. Man is an active participant in miracles.

We must make our lives fertile for the cultivation of miracles. We must strive to attune ourselves with the Father, hear His instructions, act on His guidance, grow and learn in the White Light of Spirit.

Merle Stein says, "We create our lives . . . We are our choices and our choices not made . . . We ourselves are the fountain and the feast . . ." What a beautiful expression of faith. Believe deeply enough and passionately enough in something and you will be moved to take action to obtain it and receive it.

The great man, Norman Vincent Peale, tells us, "A man who is self-reliant, positive, optimistic and undertakes his work with the assurance of success magnetizes his condition. He draws to himself the creative powers of the universe." And George Bernard Shaw puts it this way: "People are always blaming their circumstances for what they are. I don't believe in circumstances. The people who get on in this world are the people who get up and look for the circumstances they want, and, if they can't find them, make them."

How exciting to encounter these truths and to know how basically they apply to our everyday lives. We must eagerly await the wonderful circumstances in store for us, and how great the anticipation of opportunities made clear and destiny beckoning!

But how do we get this knowledge? How do we *know* what it is we want? What do we *do* to make it come about?

One way is the use of affirmations and color energy.

□ *SETTING THE STAGE* □

We're getting down in the short rows now, narrowing the focus and preparing to put the information we've learned about affirmations and color energy to use. The object of this game is to use thought energy, creative visualization, color energy, spoken word energy, and the positive energy of the cosmos to work for our personal success.

First we must set the stage.

□ *THE CANDLE FLAME* □

While we recommend the use of color energy in every possible facet of life, beginners will find the use of colored candles very effective and beautiful too!

The first use of candles is the flame itself. The flame is a focusing agent. As a partial disclaimer, please understand that our suggestion to use the flame in this fashion is not to practice self-hypnosis. Don't try to go into a trance by staring into the flame like Svengali with his mesmerizing eyes. Don't strive for an out-of-body, deep-meditation state. Simply use the candle flame to concentrate your thoughts on the business at hand.

□ *BECOME A STARE BEAR* □

Remember campfire flames? Remember how relaxing it was to sit around the campfire, speaking in soft voices, enjoying nature and night sky? Think about the warmth a fireplace generates at home: the flames leap and dance, and the mood inspired is contemplative and tranquil. Coincidentally, the word fireplace is derived from the Latin term meaning focus.

Become a stare bear. Allow the flame to float away those churning little thoughts and those gnatlike botherances of daily life. Acknowledge them and float them upward in the flame.

Begin to visualize a blank slate or a white movie screen.

As the candle flame gently wafts in the air around you, visualize your success picture piece by piece, the picture you want your mind to develop and make manifest in your life. Use the sensory skills you've learned and paint that desire—picture with broad strokes of color and fine strokes of detail on the white screen. See it completely with all minute details perfectly sketched. See action and movement. Feel emotions. Make that picture perfect.

Now, every time you gaze into a candle flame, it will remind you of that picture. Never permit your picture to fade. Every time you see the candle flame, allow that wonderful, successful, loving mind picture to spring full-blown in your mind's eye. Make a conscious statement that the flame reminds you of your mind picture. Say aloud, "The flame reminds me of my love relationship . . . my beautiful body . . . my abundant wealth."

□ *SIZES, SCENTS, AND SHAPES* □

It doesn't matter what size your candle is, or if it is scented or shaped like a Christmas tree or a Thanksgiving turkey. It is the color and the flame that is important. Votive candles are inexpensive and glass cups come in whatever color you need—the flame brings the colors alive. A red votive candle in a sparkling ruby-colored cup is beautiful, but a giant bayberry scented pillar or taper candle is just as effective.

Candles with scent are bonuses. Many times fragrance works to remind us of the mind picture. Jasmine, magnolia, carnation, or rose scents might enhance the love relationship picture. Evergreen, pine, or bayberry could remind us of nature's glory, while spice-scented (cinnamon, cloves, allspice) candles stimulate another memory. If the scent enhances the mind picture, by all means use it.

The place where you affirm does not have to smell

like Morocco or be decorated in some oriental flavor. The idea is to create a place of peace, a place where you attend to yourself and your life. So, if you enjoy incense or scented candles, or any of the other fragrance mechanisms, feel free to wax rhapsodic. Folklore tells us that some oriental monks believed that incense smoke carried their prayers to God.

□ *ATMOSPHERE* □

If music distracts, don't use it. There is a wealth of New Age music on the market today, some with nature sounds, synthesizers, violins, pianos, and the like. Pick a music which is soothing but drowns out distractions. Look for music which requires no energy to enjoy.

Gentle harmonies make relaxation easier. In harmony there is pleasure, and some music enhances the healing rhythms of the universe. Music evokes a harmonious response which speeds the reunification of man with the Father.

One of the authors uses guitar instrumentals, mostly full chords and no melody line, with a slow steady beat and no sudden increases or decreases in volume. The other author always plays piano solos accompanied by nature sounds, mostly sea waves. Your choice should be music which is gentle, spiritual, soft, and comforting.

□ *CLOTHING* □

You do not need robes. It is not necessary to buy any garment for this program; just be comfortable. Barefoot is nice, but if your feet get cold, wear socks. Take off that lovely but binding belt and get rid of that cute skirt if you must hold your stomach in. Pull on your sweat suit. Wear something comfortable and relaxing. Take off your glasses or contact lenses if they bother you, and loosen your tie or ponytail. Unplug the phone.

Position your candles, not in any special way—this is not a ritual—but where you can see them easily.

Music, candles, atmosphere: these are small things, but what you are about to experience is the beginning of a wonderful journey. Savor even the small events, like choosing music to accompany your candle burning and affirmations. Marshal your resources and remain focused—you are embarking on a program which will change your life.

□ *PUT THE WORLD ON HOLD* □

Did you know that every day 85 percent of the people in the world do nothing just for themselves, something just for selfish personal pleasure? Why this is criminal! In order to function at full potential, man must begin from a strong center or foundation. The fifteen minutes spent with candles and affirmations ought to be performed whether or not anything else gets accomplished! If man erupts from sleep into consciousness and does not focus his energy and channel his effort, every task is attempted with a shotgun splash of energy. It is wasted, and the completed task leaves a bad taste, it doesn't satisfy.

So put the world on hold. Pause for a time and nurture your energy. Very few things are so much of an emergency that delaying the task for fifteen minutes will cause chaos. Besides, we need to be good to ourselves every day. We live in an age of incredible stress, fear, and frustration, and any simple, healthy act we can do for ourselves helps heal us.

As you suspend daily operations for a time, concentrate on relaxation. It is when human bodies are relaxed that the subconscious is accessed. Work on the systematic release of muscular tension and emotional anxieties. Grace Cooke, in her book *Meditation*, encourages relaxation. "Pause in the rush of outer life and give yourself time to think and feel, so that the door of your inner consciousness may open and you can courageously seek help from the Master of your inner temple."

Start with a few short, sharp breaths to reduce tension in the body, then breathe deeply in through the nose and out through the mouth. Slow, measured breaths relax the torso and feed plenty of oxygen to all parts of the body.

Imagine a sack of corn: open the sack and let the corn pour out. You are the sack. Slowly. Slowly. Everything in slow motion.

Now you are ready to commence your affirmations. Let 'er rip.

CHAPTER VI

THE SELF

□ *SELF-LOVE* □

Oh, yes. You must love yourself. If you hate yourself, or don't even like yourself, all your energy is spent in trying to endure the heavy, heavy weight of life. Self-hate makes you do despicable things, icky nasty things which only make your happiness spiral downward, to finally blink out like a stepped-on Christmas light. If you don't like who you are and what you stand for, make it right. Become somebody you'd want to know and someone you'd want to be a part of your life. Stand for ideals and principles that are good and honorable and reasonable. Become a whole, functioning, healthy, happy human being. It is in your power to do this—read the beginning chapters of this book again and find the special person inside you.

Light a Rose candle and recite these affirmations every day.

THANK YOU, FATHER, FOR THIS WONDERFUL VESSEL IN WHICH I TRAVEL THROUGH MY LIFE. I SING GRATEFUL PRAISES FOR THE BLESSEDNESS OF MY LIFE AND ITS UNLIMITED OPPORTUNITIES!

MY HEART SWELLS AS I CONTEMPLATE THE WONDER

OF MY LIFE—NO MATTER WHAT HAS GONE BEFORE, TODAY IS MY NEW BEGINNING.

I REJOICE IN THIS NEWNESS OF LIFE. I MOVE UPWARD STEADILY, TAKING CARE OF ALL THE PRECIOUS PARTS OF MYSELF.

I HAVE REASON, PURPOSE, SELF-ESTEEM. I AM WORTHY OF BEING HAPPY. I CHOOSE TO LOVE MYSELF. I CHOOSE TO BE HAPPY.

□ *SELF-UNDERSTANDING* □

Understanding the self requires the same devotion to truth as the search for understanding others. Self-knowledge is necessary for your very survival. For successful, happy people, the goal of self-understanding is of primary importance. Identify what motivates you, what capabilities you possess, what obstacles are blocking your success. Until you understand that the Kingdom is yours, but you have to ask for it and be ready to receive it, then all success and happiness is truly out of reach.

Blue energy clears the way for self-understanding. It illuminates your strengths and powers. It minimizes your weaknesses. Human beings must understand that a few weaknesses or lack of skill in some areas are not moral sins; all people possess weaknesses, but they are not necessarily used as stumbling blocks to happiness.

Benje knew she'd never acquire the knowledge or intricate skills necessary for her to become an astronaut although that was her dearest fantasy. Benje delved into self-understanding, and soon she discovered that not becoming an astronaut was okay with her. She got her pilot's license and took some aerospace communications classes. Now Benje revels in her career in space communications—she's good at it too. Her job allows her to stretch herself, to learn new things and create. She feels valuable and worthy.

Blue rays provide an energy base for understanding the self. It does not inflame the personality to its faults, but it enlightens inherent strengths and shows the way for future happiness. Blue gives spiritual guidance in the quest for self-understanding.

I KNOW MYSELF, FATHER, AND I THANK YOU FOR THE MARVELOUS PERSON I AM. I SEE CLEARLY WITH A LOVING EYE.

I HAVE STRENGTHS, AMBITION, AND KNOWLEDGE. I AM NOT AFRAID TO KNOW WHAT I KNOW ABOUT MYSELF. I'M A PRETTY DECENT HUMAN BEING.

THE WAY IS CLEARED OF UNDERBRUSH—NO BARRIERS EXIST IN MY QUEST FOR SELF-UNDERSTANDING.

□ *SELF-AWARENESS* □

A primary mission of life is to remove all blocks so that the Father may enter and transform us into His Likeness. The barriers we erect may be removed by getting and remaining in touch with who we really are. Once we recognize and accept that we are God-made and created in His image, it becomes clear that our weaknesses and misfortunes are our own doing. Each of us is unique, endowed by the Father with special talents and abilities. Let's decide right now to kick a few of those obstructions out of the way, reveal a few new talents, and move closer to the Light of the Father. We begin through awareness.

Look within and identify what you value most. Discover which attributes you revere in yourself, like honesty or compassion. Nourish these traits and keep them healthy through action. Demonstrate honesty and compassion in your thoughts, words, and actions. If justice in relationships is of prime importance to you, then find ways of demonstrating justice in your own life. Or cherishing the earth may be shown by conscientious care of your own environment.

What the future holds for each of us is dependent upon what we do in the present. Look for and learn to use your inner potential; it is never too late to learn about yourself and to lovingly care for that singular self.

The Father is keenly aware of your individuality and He delights in us when we nourish ourselves and our aptitudes. What glory we send Him when we power ourselves forward and use a talent or ability to its greatest potential. It is up to us to discover, manifest, and perfect His gifts to us.

Since Green is representative of the commingling of man and his spirituality, this energy can help us define and enlighten our self-awareness. By concentrating on the Green rays, we move closer to alignment—harmony—and are able to reach a level of divine revelation. The emanations from Green help reveal your own particular divine plan, for each of us possesses one. Being grounded in the present, seeing visions of the possible future, and learning from the past is Green's contribution to our lives.

Spend a few quiet moments in the lush Green forest; surround yourself with inexpensive Green growing plants; lie in the grass and enjoy nature's bounty. Tune in to yourself and hear your special rhythm. Feel no constraint when you nourish your talents and aptitudes; Green is the light of self-awareness and self-nourishment.

THANK YOU, FATHER, FOR THE MANY BLESSINGS OF LIFE—YOU ARE THE GIVER OF EVERY GOOD AND PERFECT GIFT. MY MIND IS ASTOUNDED AT MY OWN TALENTS, ABILITIES, CHARACTERISTICS!

I SEE WITH A SUBLIME INNER EYE. I STRETCH MY-

SELF TO LEARN MORE ABOUT ME. I AM A FINE SPECIMEN, FATHER, A MARVELOUS WORK AND A WONDER.

I NOURISH MY INNER SPIRIT; I TAKE GOOD CARE OF MYSELF. ALL BARRIERS TO MY OWN SELF-AWARENESS ARE REMOVED, AND I GAZE UPON THE PERFECT LIFE—MY OWN.

□ *SELF-ESTEEM* □

How you regard yourself is self-esteem. The concept of self-esteem is all wrapped up in self-image, self-confidence, self-assurance, and self-acceptance. Healthy self-esteem is the means to the ends of these self things. The importance of a good self-image made possible by healthy self-esteem is that you tend to act out in life according to the picture you hold of yourself—your actions will spring directly from the emotional center which dictates what is appropriate for you. That is, whatever you feel yourself to be deep down is what you really are, and your actions will be in harmony with that feeling.

You can change your self-image, and this change can be affected by bolstering, analyzing, or reevaluating your self-esteem. You can always change the opinion you hold of yourself. It is necessarily a private, individual effort. If you get a mental picture of the person you'd like to be, and you hold this picture in your mind long enough, you will become that person.

An old self-image dies hard, but if you are strongly motivated, the new self-image will assert itself. With perseverance, you can change negative self-esteem to positive self-esteem, thereby generating success and happiness. Poor or weak self-esteem colors your entire life, and every particle of your being is affected by your own poor self-esteem. And vice versa.

We can make it almost impossible to succeed by clinging to the old negativity. Self-esteem is a powerful force, fueled by hidden capabilities and buried positive beliefs. Overcoming a poor self-image and obtaining positive self-esteem is a difficult job, but Violet energy helps.

Violet raises the consciousness above the material plane and encourages an intangible growth inside. Violet's rays illumine the self-image and point out ways to combat self-defeating mind-sets. The Without Syndrome cannot live in Violet light.

Building self-esteem puts you on a course toward happiness and success. If your spiritual values reinforce good self-esteem, the battle is almost over. Violet energy enables human beings to rid themselves of limiting beliefs and opens the door for wonderful new possibilities for achievement and happiness.

While working on your self-image, have Violet color energy around. As you gaze into the mirror and analyze who you are, wear something Violet, have violet candles burning, and decorate with violet accessories. At work, slip a picture cut from a magazine done predominantly in Violet colors between the glass and the desktop, and let this remind you of your new quest, the quest for healthy self-esteem and a good self-image.

I RID MY INNER BEING OF NEGATIVE CHARACTERISTICS. I MANIFEST GOOD SELF-ESTEEM IN MY LIFE. I DO NOT PARTICIPATE IN SELF-SABOTAGE.

THANK YOU, FATHER, FOR THE COURAGE TO CHANGE MY LIFE . . . FOR THE STRENGTH TO FACE THE CHALLENGES OF MY LIFE WITH FAITH. I MAKE GOOD DECISIONS BASED ON TRUE SELF-KNOWLEDGE.

THANK YOU, FATHER, FOR THE ESSENCE OF "ME," FOR THE COMPETENCE, CAPABILITIES, AND TALENTS THAT ARE MINE. I AM FILLED WITH GOOD SELF-ESTEEM.

□ *SELF-RESPECT* □

Personal worth. Sense of value. Pride. Dignity. Inner confidence.

All these words and phrases help explain the concept of self-respect. In order to make yourself worthy to live, you must make yourself competent to live; competence is an avenue toward good self-respect. As you grow, develop a comfortable feeling about being who you are, including frailties as well as strengths. Rose color energy provides an atmosphere conducive to this identification process. Rose—this kind, gentle energy—enables human beings to accept and respect themselves. Being able to accept and like yourself in spite of frailties and because of strengths is healthy self-respect. Rose color energy enhances this activity.

If you don't work for NASA but you make a mean tunnel-of-fudge cake, feel good about it! Anybody who tastes that cake will feel plenty good about it. Even if you can't play Rhett in *Gone With the Wind*, you might knock home runs for your softball team.

Know the good qualities about yourself and strengthen those; if you have a fault that you can't bear to demonstrate a moment longer, change it. Feel good about yourself: that is self-respect.

THANK YOU, FATHER. I LIKE ME. I'M A SWELL PERSON AND I KNOW IT. I'M OKEYDOKEY AS A HUMAN BEING.

I TREAT MYSELF WELL, FATHER, FOR I APPRECIATE THE PRECIOUSNESS OF MY LIFE. I THINK WELL OF MYSELF BECAUSE IT PLEASES YOU—AND IT PLEASES ME TOO!

I GLOW, I SHINE, I SING A SONG OF JOY—THANK YOU, FATHER, FOR MY LIFE!

□ *SELF-DEVELOPMENT* □

Self-development is a natural process of growth and differentiation. To develop, to evolve, is necessary for life. From birth, human beings develop toward maturity. Hopefully, as we develop physically, we also mature emotionally and spiritually. From basic thought processes like knowing good from evil, right from wrong, we have the highest responsibility to move forward in the acquisition of skills, creativity, knowledge, contribution, and love.

Using reason as the guide and rational behavior as the standard, human beings move from the simple to the complex, understanding each step of the way. We strive to shore up basic strengths and master difficulties and do away with self-limiting mind-sets. Again, it is the highest responsibility of all human beings to develop the inherent talents and capabilities we are born with.

Blue energy fuels us onward in this development process. Its rays emit a clean energy, one that allows clear vision and a sharp intellect. Blue matches physical, emotional, mental, and spiritual responses to outward stimuli and promotes understanding of self and of others. Blue is the color of self-development.

I SPOT MY TALENTS AND APTITUDES. I FOCUS MY ENERGY ON DEVELOPING THOSE ATTRIBUTES.

THANK YOU, FATHER, FOR ILLUMINATION, FOR KNOWLEDGE, AND THE ABILITY TO DEVELOP MY GIFTS.

I SHINE, I GLOW WITH POSSIBILITIES. I FLY HIGH AND SOAR TOWARD ACHIEVEMENT, INDEPENDENCE, CONTRIBUTION, AND HAPPINESS.

□ *SELF-CONFIDENCE* □

Walking close beside suspicion and insecurity are the gargoyles lack of confidence and inferiority. Confidence is that certainty within us that says "you can do it," "you can handle it," and "go for it." Don't ever again label yourself as inferior because this is what that word means: low-grade, second-class, mediocre, paltry, unworthy. Ugly words.

Many problems stem from lack of knowledge, and thankfully, a lack of knowledge is the easiest thing in the world to fix. A lack of self-confidence and the old inferiority complex simply disappear in the light of knowledge. When we know ourselves (yes, we've said this many times before), we pinpoint our strengths and find out where to shore up our weaknesses. With this self-knowledge, inferiority complexes weep themselves into puddles and sluice down the drainspouts of life. Do not speak the words "I am inferior" because your mind seeks to develop the picture your words paint.

And so what if you aren't adequate for a certain job? It's no sin not to know everything in the universe. We cannot excel in everything we attempt. Don't yield to depression or poor-me, but use Violet color energy to concentrate on your good abilities. Don't run away simply because the job looks hard and you have a qualm or two about being adequate for it. One of the authors has been heard to say, a mite facetiously, "The harder it gets, the better I like it." That means that every situation is an opportunity to learn more, to stretch, to gain knowledge, and to overcome cowardice. Violet encourages us to try. So what if you fall on your face? A defeat is not permanent and if you feel good about yourself, it should not diminish your capacity for life-living in the slightest.

The person who is confident in his own abilities and judges himself equal to any challenge lives a creative, fulfilling, stimulating existence. Violet color energy helps.

I AM COMFORTABLE WITH MYSELF AND MY ABILITIES. I AM FREE OF INFERIORITY FEELINGS. I AM FREE TO LIVE LIFE FULLY AND COMPLETELY. CONFIDENCE IS MY MIDDLE NAME.

I AM EQUAL TO THE CHALLENGE—I RELISH THE OPPORTUNITY!

THANK YOU, FATHER, FOR MY STRENGTH, MY DEPTH, MY REACH. I MEET LIFE'S MYRIAD SITUATIONS EAGERLY. LET THEM COME!

□ *SELF-DIGNITY* □

People don't change when they feel good. They change when they're fed up. And their actions show it. If you haven't been too jazzed up about the way you've been feeling about yourself, and you wish to work on your self-image, then use your manner to aid you. Depict self-dignity; act with the certainty that yours is the battle for whatever grandeur and joy exists on the earth, and that you are entitled to it.

Acting with dignity is not a social duty nor is it a convenient facade. It is a way of life. It is an emanation from your being; self-dignity communicates that you are worthy of the respect of others, that you possess stature and merit, and that you hold to the highest ethical standards in every area of your life. Personal dignity is not what you say or how you look—it is the essence of who you are.

Violet energy enables human beings to project an image of self-respect. This thin, light energy buzzes with spiritual power. Violet reminds us that we have poise, pride, and quality . . . that we act from a healthy self-image in daily living.

These rays give man his stature. Man's standing in the universe is clothed in Violet energy and his heroic potential is illumined. Act according to your good self-image and manifest good self-esteem. This is possible through Violet color energy.

I AM DEVOTED TO THE HIGH STANDARDS I HOLD. IN EVERY ASPECT OF MY LIFE, I ACT WITH DIGNITY AND PRIDE.

THANK YOU, FATHER, FOR THE POWER TO RULE MY SITUATION WITH HONOR AND JUSTICE. THANK YOU FOR HIGH IDEALS AND WORTHY PRINCIPLES.

I ATTAIN THE SUPREME GOAL OF HUMAN EVOLUTION—I ACT HONORABLY WITH THE CONSCIOUS AWARENESS OF MAN'S PURPOSE IN BEING.

□ *SELF-EXPRESSION* □

Has someone ever exclaimed, as you modeled a new suit or dress, "Why, it's positively *you!*" By the garment you chose, you expressed your individuality in color and style. Another indication that you've expressed your inner self successfully by the outward wrapping is when someone says, "It suits you."

Don't be a slave to fashion, just as you should not be a slave to someone else's creed for living, standards, principles, choices, careers, and the like. Dare to express yourself through your dress, your facial expression, your home, and in every other way. Besides enabling you to feel complete and satisfied, this self-expression helps others understand who you are. Live your life in your own way and represent yourself according to your own plan.

Yellow color energy provides the strength to find exactly a genuine expression of self. It illuminates the mind and encourages the body to respond. Yellow is vital, alive, and spirited. Use Yellow in big splashes to decorate your home or office. Choose bright yellow towels for the bath or a flamboyant Yellow tie or scarf.

As you seek to know yourself, light a Yellow candle and brighten up your life with self-expression.

THANK YOU, FATHER, FOR MY UNIQUENESS—FOR THE SPECIAL QUALITIES THAT MAKE ME DIFFERENT AND SEPARATE.

I BLOOM WITH INDIVIDUALITY. I SPARKLE WITH A ZEST FOR LIFE. I AM A WONDERFUL HUMAN BEING AND I EXPRESS MYSELF DISTINCTIVELY.

□ *SELF-DISCIPLINE* □

British theologian H. P. Liddon (1829–1890) wrote, "What we do upon some great occasion will probably depend on what we are; and what we are will be the results of previous years of self-discipline." We simply must acquire self-discipline if we expect change/success/happiness to manifest in our lives. We must govern the expenditure of energy, control the direction in which we travel, make systematic plans for success, and use time meaningfully and fully. All this requires self-discipline.

Self-discipline is really a system of techniques to deal constructively with problem-solving. A problem never gets solved or a decision made if we spend energy trying to evade the responsibility. Self-discipline is the tool by which every problem is handled and every decision made. As Lady Macbeth admonishes her king to screw his courage to the sticking place, we must face up to the responsibility of life and direct ourselves.

No goal was ever met without well-developed self-discipline. This characteristic has been called "stick-to-it-iveness," or perseverance. It involves the capacity to overcome rejection and other obstructions on the path to success, all the while keeping the eyes glued to the goal.

When we began the search for a literary agent to represent us, we suffered many rejections. Some agents ignored us and some, we could guess from their letters to us, were snickering in the background at our sagacity and ignorance. But we kept at it. We wrote and sent our dog-eared manuscripts out time and again, only to receive "No thanks, not my field," and "Not interested," and other less complimentary phrases. Then we found our agent. She said she'd take a look. She did and she told us she'd be proud to represent us. And, presto, several months later she placed our book idea with one of the big boys of publishing. Again, our editor championed our first manuscript but was unable to publish it; she liked it and she liked us, but she couldn't get the project accepted. Then when our agent sent the outline of this book, our editor shifted into overdrive. The result is this book, for which we will be forever grateful to our undaunted agent and editor.

Through perseverance, thick skins, and a burning desire to achieve goals, you may accomplish anything you set out to do. Your self-discipline must be sharp and ready to work.

Indigo is the energy for self-discipline. This fine vibration speaks to the mind in a spiritual way, an enlightening way that reminds us how far we can go if we stick to it. The Thwart Monster hates a person with self-discipline—he can't get a chokehold on a personality when self-discipline stands in the way. It frustrates the poor Thwart Monster and he stomps away in disgust. Deep Indigo says keep on, long after you think you've run out of energy. These rays soothe the warrior and encourage him to tap unused strength within. Indigo has great depth and strong vibrations.

When you tackle a project of immense proportions, alert the self-discipline command headquarters. Get prepared. Soap the saddle and sharpen the sword. Call up emotional strength forged in the fires of spiritual truth. Make a commitment, a solemn promise to follow through. Depend on your sovereign, rational mind. See yourself as a Knight of the Round Table, proudly astride your war steed, with a deep Indigo cape fluttering behind you as the wind whips your face. See your goal clearly in your mind, alight with Indigo rays.

I STICK TO IT, FATHER, I FIGHT ON. I DO NOT FEAR REJECTION OR DEFEAT. MY STRENGTH CARRIES ME FORWARD.

I DO NOT GIVE UP. WHATEVER IT TAKES, I KNOW THAT TODAY WILL PASS AND TOMORROW WILL COME. I PRACTICE SELF-DISCIPLINE IN EVERY ASPECT OF MY LIFE.

I AM NOT A QUITTER, I AM A STAYER. THANK YOU, FATHER, I AM VICTORIOUS.

□ *SELF-ACCOMPLISHMENT* □

Know how to set and achieve personal goals? Choose a small one, make a plan, and proceed with it; sweep away limiting mind-sets, then pat yourself on the back. If you work this infallible system, you don't have time to fail, and any defeat is only temporary. It is necessary to healthy self-esteem that you accomplish something every day . . . that you can point to something you've done or thought or figured out or said, and know that you haven't been just marking time and that you are not just taking up space on the planet.

Go back and read the chapters on motivation and goal-setting and see if you can't accomplish something just for yourself today. If you can keep from biting your fingernails for twenty minutes, that's self-accomplishment; if you rearrange the furniture in your living room, that's self-accomplishment; if you discover a cure for cancer, that too is self-accomplishment.

The energy for self-accomplishment is Red. These rays not only raise the spirit and energize the body, they spur the mind to expand and explore. Red emits a pulsing light that communicates "All is possible; all is achievable." Red color energy is a veritable warehouse of movement, action, and vitality.

When you've set a goal and made a plan to achieve it, use Red's energy to help you along. When you tackle a project, make yourself a Red badge of courage, wear a string of Red beads, work on a table covered with a Red cloth, clothe yourself in Red. Now every time you notice a splash of Red color anywhere, it will remind you that your quest is self-accomplishment, and that you have the energy available to get the job done.

Now you know. Light a Red candle for energy, determination, and stamina, and say these affirmations:

THANK YOU, FATHER, FOR I AM JOYFUL, HARMONIOUS, AND FILLED WITH LIGHT! I SET GOALS. I ACCOMPLISH THEM—ONLY ME, FATHER, BY MYSELF.

I AM A CALDRON OF BOILING IDEAS. I AM A CHARGED LIGHTNING BOLT READY TO STRIKE. I PERSIST IN MY QUEST FOR ACHIEVEMENT!

FROM MY SELF-ACCOMPLISHMENT I MAKE MYSELF WORTHY OF HAPPINESS, HEALTH, KNOWLEDGE, AND ALL GOOD THINGS. I DESERVE SUCCESS. I SUCCEED.

□ *SELF-PITY* □

The Thwart Monster dearly loves someone who feels sorry for himself. He thrives on this icky, sticky, nasty mind-set and finds fertile ground in which to cultivate the Without Syndrome seeds. Self-pity is a self-defeating attitude, and it is difficult to cure because the patient usually does not want to be cured: he'd rather wallow around and enjoy poor mental, physical, emotional, and spiritual health than put forth the effort to get over it. Self-pity manifests itself in melancholy, sad, miserable, dejected, woebegone, morose, and dismal behavior. And if we accept the tenet that we are, in a very real sense, the product of our attitudes, and if we think we are doomed, then we probably are.

Self-pity promotes self-doubt and provides the necessary energy to dwell on real or imagined inadequacies. The person awash in self-pity thinks of himself all the time, he concentrates on his weaknesses, and holds negativity as a holy creed. And remember: whatever you give energy to becomes real. The most dangerous aspect of self-pity is the possibility of losing your sense of self. If you lose the essence of your being, you become withdrawn, you criticize yourself and the world in general mercilessly, and you can never be self-sufficient. You cannot stand on your own because self-pity feeds off the attention of others to the plight of poor-little-me.

Self-pity is a highly manipulative behavior, requiring coarse, negative energy. Violet rays wipe out tacky little behaviors like self-pity. This energy will not tolerate attempts to solicit verification of man's frailties; it does not dwell on weaknesses and dependence. Violet color energy catapults man from the swamps of self-perpetuated misery and awakens the power to overcome pessimism, cynicism, sarcasm, apathy, defensiveness, and compulsive fears. This spiritual essence blots out self-pity and the behavior it demands.

I'M NOT A WHIMPERING, WHINING, SELF-PITYING WORM! I HAVE VALUABLE TALENTS AND ABILITIES! I POSSESS UNPLUMBED DEPTHS OF POWER!

THANK YOU, FATHER, FOR THE ENERGY TO PULL MYSELF OUT OF THE SLOUGH OF DESPOND AND INTO THE BRIGHT LIGHT OF LIFE. THANK YOU FOR THE WIDER VISION OF THE UNIVERSE.

I AM EFFECTIVE, STRONG, AND CAPABLE. I DO NOT GIVE THE KISS OF DEATH TO MY HAPPINESS THROUGH SELF-PITY. I SHINE WITH GOOD HEALTH.

CHAPTER VII

SPIRITUAL HEALTH

□ *FAITH* □

Faith is a surety of knowing that sees and recognizes the power that brings accomplishment and looks beyond all boundaries to transcend all limitations. It demolishes all obstacles and sees the goal; it never fails. You have heard that all is possible to him who believes. Faith is not a wish. It is a creative force that makes things happen, a catalyst which sets events in motion. Only people who possess a strong faith in themselves and their importance to the universe achieve goals. People who demonstrate this kind of faith enable others to seek faith also. A leader who practices a deep and abiding faith in himself, his universe, and the Higher Power lives an enlightened life, driven by the divine conception of absolute happiness.

Blue helps find and/or renew faith. Its spiritual glow lights up the dark corners of life and spotlights inner faith. Blue rays strengthen this inner faith. Without faith, life becomes a meaningless scramble, with no focus and no clear goals. Unless totally by accident, no one ever accomplished anything without a plan, a mental success picture, and faith in the power to develop that picture. Blue is positive faith; it is the direct opposite of fear. As such, Blue energy working to strengthen faith empowers man's will to achieve.

Faith is the springboard of will, the starting block of achievement.

Within the Blue light of the spectrum, faith can also heal emotional and spiritual setbacks. Disappointment, failed expectations, and unreasonable goals may wound, but they are righted with Blue energy, allowing man to know that adjustment, not surrender, is the answer to those wounds. Mary, the mother of Christ, is oftentimes painted in pale Blue, the Blue energy of pure faith.

I NEVER DOUBT. I NEVER WASTE ENERGY IN NEGATIVITY. I BELIEVE.

THANK YOU, FATHER, FOR EVERY SPECK AND PARTICLE OF MY EXISTENCE, AND FOR YOUR STRENGTHENING PRESENCE IN MY EVERY ENDEAVOR.

I CAN. I WILL. I DO. I ACCOMPLISH. I BELIEVE.

□ *WILL* □

The embodiment of will is pure faith in action, jump-started by the energy of faith and the alignment of man's will with the Father's. Will is what drives man to achievement. Creativity is achieved by man's will. Money and worldly riches are achieved as one product of man's will and faith; so are happiness, success, love, and so forth. Will is what determines what you'll do with your opportunities. Faith is the knowing and will is the doing. When the door to opportunity is opened by man's faith, the will pushes him through it.

The color Blue is associated with man's will. It is through this energy that man's endowment of free will makes itself manifest throughout the physical, mental, emotional, and spiritual selves. Blue is the symbol of the power of spirit. Man's focused will has a determination and persistence to achieve his purpose no matter what obstacles arise. Blue allows man to know and believe in his personal power.

You've probably heard people say, with a huge sigh of resignation, "It's God's Will." This seems to be an excuse for failure, defeat, giving up, self-pity, and shame. When this phrase is uttered, are we blaming God for bad things that happen? If we believe that the Father wants us to be happy and successful, why would He send defeat to us as His Will? Doesn't make sense. When man's will is aligned with the Father's Will, nothing stands in the way—everything is possible—and success is a paralyzed fact. Absolute happiness is all around us and the sun shines bright again. Total joy and fulfillment are achieved when we join forces with the Father in our quest for happiness and productivity.

Blue is the spirit ray: it lifts, exalts, and inspires man to greater heights of enlightenment. As man's spirit is lifted upward, we soar like eagles, powered by will and spurred onward by faith. We become enraptured with the beauty and blissfulness of life; we delight in life itself. Blue is the color energy of will.

I THRILL TO THE POWER OF MY WILL. I AM READY TO BURST FORTH IN A CREATIVE, PRODUCTIVE FERVOR OF ACTIVITY.

FATHER, YOUR WILL IS MY WILL. I FOLLOW YOUR DIRECTIONS—WITH A GRATEFUL HEART, I ACHIEVE HAPPINESS, SUCCESS, AND ENLIGHTENMENT.

□ *PURPOSE* □

If you have spent some time in becoming aware of yourself, you will probably have little difficulty in determining your purpose in life. Since we've all been given different gifts, it is up to us to mesh those attributes with our newfound self-knowledge. (Incidentally, the perfect combination of your gifts with your talents and the culmination of that activity to achieve optimum production is that radiant state of being known as success.)

Our daily lives are the programs of our own creation. How we react to some stimuli is a learned response while some responses are instinctive. We can shape those learned responses to our liking. If you see a beautiful sunset, do you immediately want to draw or paint it? Do you want to photograph it? Do you simply acknowledge its beauty and savor your enjoyment? When you see a hungry child, do you search for food or is your first response one of anger at the plight of this child? Do you want to take action and rage at the world or do you meet the child's immediate need? Do you fix the short-term problem and then consider the long-term outcome, or do you cogitate upon the long-term and counsel patience and caution for the short-term answer?

By the identification of our instinctive and learned responses, we may find a purpose for our lives. Are you a builder or a philosopher? Hopefully you are a builder-philosopher. Your purpose in life will become known when you make a concerted effort to find out what it is.

Green is the conduit of spiritual knowledge to our own human ears. Through this energy, harmony and balance can be attained, the successful interfacing of physical and spiritual. Energy emitted by Green is a natural starting place for identifying purpose and climbing aboard the success horse of life.

Maybe you have more than one purpose; maybe you have several miniature purposes and one maxipurpose. And maybe your purpose is not so grand-sounding as world peace or the cure of cancer, but your purpose—and know this with your whole being—is just as important and necessary to you as anybody else's in the world. Green energy will flood you with calm strength and confidence and, in its light, you will be able to find your mission.

I AM AN IMPORTANT PART OF THIS GLORIOUS WORLD. I HAVE SOME NECESSARY "SOMETHING" THE WORLD REQUIRES. I AM STILL AND I LISTEN TO MY INNER SELF. I FIND MY PURPOSE.

THANK YOU, FATHER, FOR THE REVELATION OF MY DIVINE PLAN FOR LIFE. I UNDERSTAND MY RESPONSIBILITY FOR MY OWN FUTURE. I CAN'T WAIT TO FIND MY PURPOSE AND BEGIN MY JOURNEY!

□ *OPEN YOUR CHANNEL! EXPAND YOUR MIND!* □

It is known that human beings use only a fraction of the mind's power. We can better utilize this power by consciously and deliberately enlarging our capacity for knowledge. Life itself is ready to share resources with us; we have only to decide and ask.

Life begets life. You can choose to hang out in the same old place, or you can choose to be forever moving toward the Light: always eager to learn something new, to try and experiment, to stretch your capacity for action. In Yellow's light, we embrace life's myriad functions. Don't be afraid to live your life! Let your mental faculties become stimulated and restless, powered by Yellow's limitless mental energy.

Start right now to begin afresh. Close your eyes and bask in the humming Yellow rays of the sun. Get ready! Can you feel your mind beginning to expand? Can you feel your energy level rising, ready to unfold some new facet of your individuality?

Get after it! Let it come! Let Yellow color energy

power you toward the ideal: becoming a clear and perfect open channel for your spirituality.

I'M READY, FATHER! FILL ME, FLOOD ME, ENERGIZE ME! I AM A CLEAR AND PERFECT OPEN CHANNEL FOR SPIRITUAL KNOWLEDGE!

THANK YOU, FATHER, FOR THE LIMITLESS CAPACITY OF MY MIND, AND THE FUEL TO DRIVE ME FORWARD TOWARD ENLIGHTENMENT.

OPPORTUNITIES UNFOLD—I EXPAND—I AM MAGNIFIED—MY BRAIN IS CROWDED WITH NEW IDEAS!

□ *ENTHUSIASM* □

Uplifted spirits will carry you far up the road to success. An eagerness to face whatever comes your way defeats dread and worry. If you know exactly what's going to happen, what you need and want to do (and even if you don't!), be enthusiastic—high spirits can make a drudgery bearable.

Enthusiasm is a natural companion for Red's exciting energy. Red's natural effect on human beings is instantaneous and dramatic; it emboldens one who is shy, it energizes those who need mind fuel, and it diminishes fear and anxiety.

When you face a new opportunity or a new challenge and need your spirits uplifted, light a Red candle to increase enthusiasm. Red is the fuel you need in order to rise to the occasion. If you feel down and dreary, put on a blouse or shirt in screaming Red. Walk around the mall and play a game with yourself: every time you see something Red in a shop window, give yourself a point for enthusiasm. When you finally count your "enthusiasm points," you will find that you have collected plenty of energy to face this exciting life.

THANK YOU, FATHER, FOR EXCITING OPPORTUNITIES AND CHALLENGES! I GROW, I LEARN, I LOVE!

MY ENTHUSIASM IS CONTAGIOUS! THROUGH MY ENERGY AND EXCITEMENT, I FACE MY LIFE AND MY WORLD WITH EAGERNESS!

I TINGLE WITH ANTICIPATION FOR WHAT LIES ROUND THE BEND! I CAN'T WAIT TO GET STARTED!

□ *INTUITION, MESSAGES, HUNCHES, AND FEELINGS* □

We've written much about intuition or mankind's sixth sense, and we cannot emphasize enough the importance of paying attention to it. It has been explained that intuition is the quality or spiritual faculty of the mind which directly perceives truth without the use of the other senses. It does not explain where it comes from or why, it only reveals. So, by intuition, you can know something without knowing how or why.

Someone once observed that intuition is given only to him who has undergone long preparation to receive it. What a novel thought, you say! But the gift of intuition is only given to those who are alert to the function. A person who deliberately disregards a hunch, goes against his better judgment, or practices denial of intuitive feelings is turning his back on a lifetime of his experience, for intuition takes its content from life itself and applies it to present day. When it is encouraged and nurtured, the subconscious uses its prodigious store of knowledge to send messages to the conscious. And the broader your experience and the more open your mind, the more likely your intuition will work effectively for your good.

The sixth sense or hunch cannot come to you if your mind is cluttered or tied in knots. The body and the mind must be relaxed and ready to receive the transmissions. If you practice receiving intuitive thoughts, they will become more numerous and more accurate.

The Father sends us, His children, constant messages. But He does not speak to our consciousness. He speaks to us through the spirit. He gives us gentle nudges, promptings, urges, and pushes. Then it is up to us to respond. Intuition has been called guidance, the inner voice, and the conscience. All intuition really is is the Father whispering to us. We must open our "ears" to hear His instructions.

Every one of us is intuitive, but some of us have concentrated on developing this semihidden power and we have become attuned to our psychic selves. What the Father has in mind for us is more than we could ever desire or pray for, so it behooves us to put ourselves in the listening mode and pay attention to our intuition.

To heighten your intuitive awareness, light an Indigo candle. Concentrate on Indigo's fine vibrations and absorb them. Picture yourself as a clear and perfect open channel for messages. Through Indigo vibrations you may open your spiritual perception and, spontaneously, the Father's wisdom will be revealed.

It is beneficial for beginning students to concentrate on a mural or wall painted deep blue-violet Indigo. The infinity of space is accorded a special significance in this lesson: through the impossible task of understanding the magnitude of the universe and its energies, we come to know that earth is not the be-all and end-all of life. Indigo vastness spreads before us as we gaze into the night sky, whizzing by stars and planets, deeper and deeper into space and into the mind. As you probe deep into yourself, Indigo's capacity for channeling intuitive messages to the conscious mind becomes a strong pulsing power.

Indigo's energy allows us entry into the deepest, most complex part of ourselves; it is the wisest and most daring ability that makes us aware of our deepest needs and highest possibilities. Indigo is cooling and electric in nature, and it is a great healing energy.

To enhance your intuitive ability, use Indigo, either by colored candle, decor accouterments, or as a contemplative tool (as in gazing at an Indigo night sky, painted mural, or a sheet tacked up on the game-room wall).

FLOOD ME, FATHER, WITH DIVINE KNOWLEDGE. WHISPER TO ME YOUR INSTRUCTIONS, MESSAGES, AND DIRECTIONS.

MY BODY, MIND, AND SPIRIT ARE ALIVE WITH DIVINE POWER. I AM ONE WITH THE UNIVERSE—A CLEAR AND PERFECT OPEN CHANNEL FOR DIVINE GUIDANCE.

ALL WISDOM, ALL POWER, ALL LOVE ARE AVAILABLE TO ME THROUGH DIVINE INTELLIGENCE. MY INTUITION SENDS ME IRREFUTABLE TRUTHS AND PERFECT INFORMATION. I RECEIVE IT LOUD AND CLEAR.

□ *ALIGNMENT WITH THE FATHER* □

Alignment of man and the Father is ultimate enlightenment. As human beings struggle to overcome inadequacies, searching for that elusive state of perfect harmony, the Father's eyes watch us all the while. Every force in the universe cheers us on. Many times the desire to align ourselves is not backed by the commitment, so when a stone blocks the path to attunement, human beings generally give up, and they snatch from the jaws of perfect bliss the opportunity to move successfully with the forces of the universe.

Alignment grants wisdom and power, for there is no force greater or no more perfect state of being than when man has become an open channel to the Father. Alignment with the Father is the brass ring, the pot of gold, the lamp in the darkness. When we are aligned with the Father, He allows us abundant power to shape our environment in pleasing, happy, successful ways. He grants us access to wisdom and knowledge, and we spontaneously grasp ways to implement this data and transform our lives for the better.

White, of course, is the color of complete alignment with the Father. Its rays are positive and its motivation pure. In White's energy, we are reminded that all things are possible when man is in harmony with the Father and His universe. No evil can exist in White's cleansing rays.

I AM AN OPEN CHANNEL TO SPIRITUAL REALIZATION. I AM ONE WITH THE FATHER.

THANK YOU, FATHER, FOR PERFECT HARMONY IN MY LIFE . . . FOR PURE LIGHT, LOVE, AND ATTAINMENT.

I RECEIVE THE HIGHEST LEVELS OF SPIRITUAL AWARENESS AND I AM COMPLETE.

□ *TOUCHING BASE WITH OUR SPIRITUAL BEING* □

Raking away the dead leaves of daily life and touching base with your spiritual being will renew the spirit and infuse new energy into life. This process is a cleansing fire which burns away triviality, meanness of spirit, petty concerns, and tacky little sins. Periodically, if we choose to become spiritual beings, a little touching base is in order; it is, in fact, necessary for inner growth.

Blue makes the perfect background for this sometimes painful but always healthy procedure. Its energy soothes and calms and promises tranquillity and the uniting of our will with the Father's benevolence. It is sad but true that usually this touching base takes place only in a crisis, and only in times of great emotional upheaval do we find the center of our spiritual being. By then, the path to our spiritual center has become clogged with old pain and guilt. Touching base with our spiritual center should be a maintenance policy. Then, in a crisis, we've got a jump on conquering the pain and confusion.

A cool Blue light speeds up and clarifies this journey. Through these rays it becomes possible to align ourselves with the Higher Power. Blue highlights vital principles by which we live and builds faith (which then builds inner strength).

ALL EARTHLY ENERGY AND STATIC FADES INTO THE BACKGROUND. MY SPIRITUAL BEING EMERGES, PULSING WITH LIFE. A SEARCHLIGHT FOCUSES ON MY VERY SELF AND I AM ILLUMINATED.

THANK YOU, FATHER, FOR YOUR PRESENCE IN THIS SOLEMN MOMENT. I ALIGN MYSELF WITH YOUR POWER AND WE ARE ONE.

□ *INNER PEACE AND HAPPINESS* □

The most comforting idea in the universe is that you are responsible for your own circumstances. Yes, comforting. Because you've created your circumstances, and if you are not happy, then you can change them. In order to achieve inner peace and happiness, do not blame others for your current situation; recognize that others do not have the power (unless you give it to them) to make you miserable: only you have that power. And, with the same power, you can decide to be happy.

Since Blue is the color of alignment, it should be present as you strive for inner peace and happiness. Blue cleanses the spirit of woe and worry, and allows the physical, emotional, mental, and spiritual selves to combine with the power of the Father. Life will then crackle with electricity and potential. Since Divine Guidance directs us to be happy people, this process will get us there.

You must give yourself permission to change, permission to feel pleasure, satisfaction, contentment, and joy. You must give yourself permission to feel calm, quiet, free, and tranquil. If you do not grant yourself these permissions, then you do not believe happiness is appropriate, and you'll subconsciously sabotage any tender seedling of happiness. Inner peace and happiness are your birthright.

Blue energy floats away destructive thoughts and shows up blocking behavior as valueless. It allows human beings to accept happiness and peace, and to strive for it in the future. Blue is cool and calm; it evokes a soothing response. Make your room into a Blue heaven, gaze into the clear Blue sky, and light your Blue candles. Get ready for wonderful feelings.

I AM RELAXED, CALM, AND PEACEFUL. I AM WORTHY OF HAPPINESS AND INNER PEACE. I GIVE MY PERMISSION FOR THESE FEELINGS TO MANIFEST IN MY LIFE.

THANK YOU, FATHER, FOR MY RADIANT STATE OF HAPPINESS. THANK YOU FOR MELTING AND DISSOLVING ANY NEGATIVE INFLUENCE. I REACH THE WONDERFUL STATE OF PEACE AND HARMONY. I LIVE MY LIFE GENTLY.

C H A P T E R VIII

MENTAL AND EMOTIONAL HEALTH

□ *ANGER* □

Anger is a basic human emotion. Many people have problems dealing with anger because it is misunderstood and frightening. If you feel angry and turn away from it, if you do not express it appropriately, it eats away at you and poisons every thought, word, and deed. The Thwart Monster is angry and you see what damage he can do! How much better it is to get anger over with in a short effective burst than to dwell on it and stew over a long period of time. Repressed anger is a self-destructive emotion; wholesome anger is not madness, but a cleansing expenditure of energy. It requires a certain inner strength to deal with anger and get by it, but we have coping tools in the mind to deal with it. We can also utilize whatever other energy is available.

Red color energy helps get anger over with in a hurry, but correctly. These rays bristle with ire and disquiet. Red opens a safe channel for the expulsion of anger. When you "see Red" and feel anger, retain control of your functions. Realize that you still possess the basic and necessary presence of mind to deal effectively with your anger. In blunter terms, if you are angry, just be angry, express it, and then shut up.

Light an angry Red candle and face the emotion. It might be a good idea to couple the Red candle with a soothing, cool color at the other end of the spectrum—this finer energy will help calm you down after your little explosion. To deal with anger in a healthy fashion, we recommend the use of candles and affirmations, followed by a period of meditation or deep relaxation.

THANK YOU, FATHER, FOR I AM STRONG ENOUGH TO FEEL ANGER AND DEAL WITH IT. I AM ANGRY, FATHER; I FEEL COMPELLED TO EXPRESS IT.

BOOM! BANG! SOCK! POW! MY ANGER DIMINISHES WITH EVERY BREATH.

AS I LOSE THE FORCE OF THIS EMOTION, MY CALM STRENGTH TAKES OVER.

THANK YOU, FATHER, FOR MY HEALTHY EXPRESSION OF ANGER.

PEACE REIGNS AGAIN IN THE TEMPLE OF MY SPIRIT. I AM PLACID, SERENE, RENEWED, AND HEALTHY.

□ *ASSERTIVENESS* □

Check out your personality and find out if you possess an abundance of any of the following: shyness, fear, discomfort, embarrassment, self-consciousness, dry mouth and sweaty palms, droopy head and furtive eyes. Do you have "doormat" tattooed on your forehead? Are you a shrinking violet? Is your surname Milquetoast?

If any of the above are true, you lack assertiveness.

Engrave this in your memory: feelings are neither right nor wrong; feelings just are. Your feelings are valid simply because they are your feelings, and as such they are valuable. Your opinions, thoughts, and emotions are just as real and important as anyone's. So don't shrink from expressing yourself or asserting your ideas and opinions whenever and wherever appropriate.

So what if somebody says something derogatory about your observations or ideas? You have just as much right as any other human being on this planet to assert your thoughts. They are genuine and authentic. And that other somebody may be full of hogwash, and the world may just be waiting with bated breath to hear your recommendations.

Stand up. Speak out. Eschew fear of ridicule. Ridicule is a paper tiger and diminishes your stature as a valuable human being not in the slightest. Put on a big Yellow hat and get ready to be counted. Whip out that bright Yellow handerchief and wave it—get folks' attention and let 'em know what you think.

Work on this aspect of your personality in private. Light a gleaming, courageous Yellow candle and speak with feeling:

I AM A POSITIVE, ASSERTIVE FELLOW. I AM NOT AFRAID TO SPEAK OUT AND LET MY THOUGHTS BE KNOWN.

THANK YOU, FATHER, FOR THE BRAVE STAND I TAKE IN THE WORLD. I TAKE CHARGE OF MY OWN SITUATION. MY IDEAS ARE VALUABLE. THE INFORMATION I POSSESS IS NEEDED BY THE WORLD.

I AM CONFIDENT, POISED, AND FILLED WITH LIGHT.

□ *COMPASSION AND SYMPATHY* □

Experience is a great teacher, the only true teacher, because we have greater, truer compassion and sympathy for someone else when we have experienced the same or similar circumstances. Quan Yin, the ancient Chinese goddess, represented compassion, and she was an important deity in daily life; the Chinese revered compassion. It is a natural impulse for human beings to feel compassionate and sympathetic to others, even though in recent times we've become hardened and closed in. Sympathy is a gift we give to another because of his circumstances or because of his struggle. Compassion begins with supportiveness. It is a balm to the soul of one who suffers.

Rose is compassion and sympathy. Its gentle energy allows us to soothe the wounded warrior with the balm of sympathy. When we are sensitive and kind toward others, we receive the same in return. Rose offers the solace so desperately needed by the sufferer.

Send a beautiful Rose-colored candle to one you care about who may be suffering. Let him know that you feel compassion and sympathy in his time of trouble. Help him to understand that you too feel his woe but that soon the sun will shine again.

THANK YOU, FATHER, FOR THE ABILITY TO FEEL COMPASSIONATE TOWARD MY FELLOWMAN. I AM SORRY FOR HIS PAIN AND SUFFERING.

I OFFER THE SOOTHING BALM OF TENDER COMPASSION TO ONE WHO SUFFERS. I FEEL, I CARE.

THANK YOU, FATHER, FOR MERCY AND KINDNESS. I DEMONSTRATE KINDLINESS, SYMPATHY, AND COMPASSION TO ONE WHO SUFFERS.

□ *COURAGE AND BRAVERY* □

The word courage is Latin in origin. It passed into English from the French word for "heart," *coeur*. When a racehorse overcomes pain and other obstacles in order to finish a race, we say he has a lot of "heart," and being brave in the face of danger truly begins in the heart of ourselves. You have more courage than you think you do: bravery comes from living through experiences. You've lived through crises when you thought all was lost and you were about finished. This is courage from the heart.

Courage requires coarse, pulsing energy, the rawest, most powerful energy you can muster. Red provides it. Light a fiery Red candle, absorb the surge of energy in its rays, and confront the scary thing. Stand tall, throw your head back, then meet and master the fear.

If you must deal with an emotional fear and must gather yourself to face it, find a quiet time to work on your mind. Make yourself or purchase a Red heart-shaped pillow and hold it close or lay your head on it. Visualize an armored knight astride his war-horse—he carries a blood-Red flag. An ancient Native American custom utilized Red color energy. Warriors carried a small Red bag filled with oak leaves for strength of mind, a wolf or bear claw for cunning and power, Red trade beads for hot blood and courage, and other items to which they assigned magical powers. Whether or not they were magic does not matter; what was important was that these talismans reminded them to demonstrate bravery and courage in battle.

Red color energy provides an extra boost of power, enough power to get you past the first twinges of fear and into the fray. These rays were meant to be used to provide courage and bravery. Red rays are bold and fearless.

THANK YOU, FATHER, FOR I DEMONSTRATE THE COURAGE OF THE LION—THE GLADIATOR—THE WARRIOR. I THROW OPEN THE DOORS OF STRENGTH IN MY HEART, AND I STAND FAST.

I AM BRAVE. I CONTROL FEAR. MY HEART BEATS SOLIDLY, FIERCELY, CONSISTENTLY.

THESE RUGGED MOUNTAINS, THESE ROLLING SEAS, THESE BLAZING FLAMES POSE NO THREAT TO ME! I AM BOLD. I AM HEROIC.

□ *DEPRESSION AND DESPAIR* □

Depression is a state of morbid unhappiness. Despair is hopeless melancholy. Depression kills initiative. Despair shuts down necessary life functions.

Depression can be caused by a chemical imbalance in the brain. If you suffer from depression, please get help from a qualified health care specialist. Depression caused by organic malfunction can be treated with medication. If left untreated, tragic consequences can occur. Get a professional opinion first, then analyze your inner self.

If you give in to depression, you've allowed the enemy to win with little effort on its part. We've said before that the enemy is apathy and passivity—the lack of action. Depression and despair are brought about by loneliness, grief, pain, and fear. There is nothing natural about dealing with problems by holding on to depression. Anger is natural; so are grief and disappointment. Despair is going belly-up and letting a train run over you. You need a giant surge of energy to move you out of the depression/despair rut, for this rut demonstrates the Without Syndrome at its best.

Blast your way out of the slough of despond! Light a big Red candle and light it *now!* Drink eagerly from Red's vitality and strength. Everywhere you look, put something Red in the direct line of sight. Fix yourself a glass of icy Red fruit punch. Stop by the florist and admire the Red roses; go shopping and try on anything Red; stick a bright Red handkerchief in your suit pocket. Red color energy acts immediately and directly on depression and despair. Even if you'd rather wallow around in it, feel sorry for yourself, and seek pity from others for your plight, it just doesn't sell if you perform these activities dressed in Red.

THANK YOU, FATHER, FOR YOUR LIGHT SHINES EVEN INTO THE DARKEST CORNERS OF MY LIFE. IN YOUR LIGHT, I FIND MY WAY.

I CAST OUT THE DEPRESSION DEMON! I BANISH DESPAIR. I TAKE ACTION! I CONQUER EVIL AND I SWEEP AWAY ALL OBSTACLES.

THE FLOODGATES OF INNER ENERGY BLAST OPEN—OUT POURS THE CHURNING POWER OF LIFE! I RIDE THE STEED OF STRENGTH AND BY MY WILL I TRIUMPH!

□ *DISAPPOINTMENT AND FRUSTRATION* □

Pat has a dead lock on dealing with disappointment and frustration, and her trick is simple. To guard against being disappointed, hold reasonable expectations. To defend against frustration, ask "who owns the problem" and "what am I in charge of?" After mastering this trick, she found she possessed greater tolerance, greater compassion, and greater understanding—what an unexpected plus!

There's no way around it: sometimes we will be disappointed, either in another person, a situation, or in ourselves. If we cling to reasonable rational expectations, we can keep disappointment at a minimum. Inevitably, when we are justifiably disappointed, wallowing around in it and toting that baggage throughout the remainder of life is counterproductive. We must let go of old disappointments and see them as stepping-stones toward achievement and happiness.

Frustration requires an immense amount of immediate energy, and it doesn't stop at that! Frustration is a self-perpetuating cannibal. It is wise to stop frustration at the first sign. Lighten up. Recognize frustration as something you cannot control in a situation in which you have no power. Waiting on events to take place causes much frustration; waiting on someone else to make a decision or take some action sends the frustration quotient through the roof. Remind yourself that what you cannot control, what you are not responsible for, is not in your arena of responsibility. The only thing you *can* do is lessen it.

Cussin' (or cursing) is often the result of frustration. Sometimes, if you go into a room by yourself and cuss a blue streak, you can get a handle on frustration. Cussin' does not have to contain profanity: you can do raspberries or Snoopy's favorite, "Aaaaaggghhhhh," or any other rude sound. The best way is just to avoid frustration by being reasonable and rational.

Orange is a loud color, one that explodes with noise and light and good humor. This energy helps us laugh at ourselves and our antics in dealing with frustration.

As far as disappointments are concerned, Orange energy helps us to get by them and find positive vibrations elsewhere. Orange enlightens expectations and lets us know what is reasonable, rational, and positive.

BIFF! BANG! SOCK! POW! I AM THE BATMAN OF FRUSTRATION, THE GREEN LANTERN OF AGGRAVATION, THE MOUNT ST. HELEN'S OF EXPLODING FRUSTRATION!

NOW IT IS OUT OF MY SYSTEM.

I MAKE THE MOST OF MY SITUATION; I HANDLE DIS-

APPOINTING SITUATIONS IN MATURE WAYS. I MEET DISAPPOINTMENT AND FRUSTRATION ON MY TERMS—THE TERMS OF REASON AND RATIONALITY.

THANK YOU, FATHER, FOR PATIENCE, TOLERANCE, AND MATURITY. I DETACH MYSELF FROM OLD DISAPPOINTMENTS . . . THEY FLOAT AWAY TO MAKE ROOM FOR ACCOMPLISHMENTS AND POSITIVE FEELINGS.

□ *FEAR* □

Fear is a powerful energy. Energy is magnetic. Whatever you fear, you magnetize and attract.

Coping with fear requires an aggressive action: walk up to it, confront it, bring it out in the open. Easier said than done, right? Well, just try it one time.

You've been offered a new job. You believe you are organizing your thoughts in order to make an educated or informed decision. But tiny little doubts and fears begin to slip in. What if I don't like it when I get there? What if the people I will be working with are awful? What if I can't do the job? What if . . . what if . . . what if . . . Pretty soon, you've gone round and round so many times, you've turned to butter.

See where you're going? Nowhere. No informed decision can be made with all those what-if gnats buzzing around. Old cowboys like to say, "Don't hunt for boogers." Don't list potential disastrous situations. Don't get trapped in the what-if swamp. Because whatever you fear, you give energy to.

Orange, with its buoyant, indomitable spirit, just won't allow you to cringe in the shadows. Orange says, "Face it!" "Look at it!" "Examine the facts!"

Orange energy helps face fear and master it. Fear of the unknown stymies most people at some point or another, but you can choose to consider a dilemma without hiding under the bleachers. You can sit in the grandstand and make your decision, then you can get in the game. Any kind of fear can be mastered if you decide you want to master it. Exuberant Orange will give you the energy you need to whip it. Can you imagine a person wearing a sparkling Orange dress hiding in the shadows? People who wear Orange just have to be fearless!

I FACE FEAR RATIONALLY. I SEE IT, IDENTIFY IT, AND MASTER IT.

THANK YOU, FATHER, FOR THE ABILITY TO TURN FEAR INTO FAITH. THANK YOU FOR MY COURAGEOUS NATURE, MY BRAVERY IN THE FACE OF DECISION, MY STRENGTH IN MAKING GOOD DECISIONS.

I SEE CLEARLY, I CONSIDER REASONABLY, I MOVE CONFIDENTLY. I MAKE GOOD DECISIONS. SHOO, LITTLE FEARS, YOU HAVE NO PLACE IN MY LIFE!

□ *FORGIVENESS* □

Unless you are the perfect person, there will be times when you, knowingly or unknowingly, commit some act that will require you to ask for forgiveness. Also, others will wound you in some way, and they will ask, or need to ask, for forgiveness from you.

Consider how much energy is necessarily required to attend to a storehouse of old wounds and wrongs. Why, you can spend your entire life picking at the scabs of past wounds, carrying grudges, and distrusting and despising whoever wrongs you! On the other side of that coin, you can spend precious time groveling in shame, begging for a crumb of absolution, or never making a move for fear of stepping on someone else's feet. Face it. We bumble through life, receiving slights and committing wrongs right and left, and there is simply nothing we can do about history but acknowledge the heinous act and forgive ourselves or forgive the wrongdoer and go on.

Rose, with its gentle, tender light, is perfect for forgiveness. Rose glows rather than glitters, and all wounds require a gentle touch. Rose raises us up from base concerns and guides us to forgive and seek forgiveness. Rose is solace and comfort, sensitivity and blessedness. Its light banishes the urge to beat the whey out of somebody else and forbids us to crawl on our bellies to others. Rose energy allows imperfect human beings to forgive and be forgiven.

Shed a tear, light your lovely Rose candle, then forgive or ask forgiveness. Once you forgive and are forgiven, put it behind you and don't look back.

THANK YOU, FATHER, FOR THE OPPORTUNITY TO RIGHT A WRONG. I ACKNOWLEDGE THE SINS OF MY PAST AND I LET THEM GO.

I FORGIVE. I ASK FORGIVENESS. I DO NOT REMAIN IN PAIN FOREVER—IT PASSES AND I COPE.

THE GENTLE BALM OF FORGIVENESS SOOTHES ME. THE GENTLE BALM OF FORGIVENESS I FREELY GIVE. I SEEK BALANCE IN FORGIVING AND IN SEEKING FORGIVENESS.

I GET BY THIS PAINFUL TIME AND MOVE ON TO A BEAUTIFUL PLACE, SOOTHED AND GENTLED.

□ *FREEDOM TO CHANGE* □

Giving yourself permission to change your life is what this book is all about. We resist change because we fear the unknown. We're afraid to change because "what if" is such a basic activity of the Thwart Monster. Once the Thwart

Monster gets loose when you are attempting to make a decision to change, you will be overwhelmed with disastrous possibilities. Instead of making a rational, reasonable, positive change, you'll hide under the bed. You'll avoid opportunities and miss out on fun, happiness, and accomplishments. When you make responsible decisions, having given yourself permission to change, you become a lot less angry at the world and with yourself.

Life is a series of reassessments of goals, needs, desires. Whether change is the kind we decide to make or if change is thrust upon us, we feel apprehensive. Change is unsettling, and we do not like to feel unbalanced. But life in its entirety is change, and we can either embrace it and dance with it, or resist it and be steamrollered. Because, whatever else happens, change is here to stay.

Orange is the color for positive change. It enlightens opportunities; it searches for good. Orange color energy blows away negative, nonproductive emotions and rids the mind of distractions. These rays increase our capacity to cope with change. They help us realize that change is part of the maturing cycle of life. Orange aids us in making both insignificant and profound decisions. In the light of this enthusiastic color, new ideas and new directions spring up unsummoned.

I ADAPT TO MY CHANGING, ENRICHING LIFE. I LOOK FORWARD TO CHANGE. MY FUTURE SHINES AS BRIGHT AS THE SUN.

THANK YOU, FATHER, FOR THE FUEL AND COMMITMENT NECESSARY TO CHANGE MY LIFE FOR THE BETTER, TO ENRICH MY WORLD, TO CONTRIBUTE TO THE GOODNESS OF THE UNIVERSE.

CHANGE IS FUN AND EXCITING, AND THE VERY BEST THING TO HAVE IS FUN!

□ *GOSSIP* □

We found it hard to write about gossip, either doing it or having it done to us, because gossip is so negative and so unnecessary. Careless conversations filled with slander and lies, innuendoes and insinuations, misrepresentations and revenge are evil. If we participate in them, we don the cloak of evil, and if we listen to them, we sanction their existence. It is a serious matter to speak an injustice about someone else, and the law of Karma will see that the speaker pays dearly for it.

If you indulge in gossip, you have indulged in the "make-me-look-better-and-larger-by-making-my-fellow-look-smaller-and-worse" game. This premise has a false bottom. By our gossip report, we may have injured an innocent person, which is a crime exacting a high penalty. On the other hand, being gossiped about diminishes the gossipee not in the least. Gossip only cheapens the ones who participate in it.

Violet energy can combat the temptation to gossip. It can also lessen the impact of it. These rays do not have time for smut peddlers who cloak their nasty conversations in a righteous "concern." Violet makes us stop and think when we are too hasty to believe an evil report.

This spiritually pure energy raises man above the tawdry words of a base character and ejects him to a plane not tainted by slander or gossip. Wear a Violet badge, pin, or ribbon; let others know you do not gossip and you will not listen to it.

I RISE ABOVE GOSSIP—IT HAS NO PLACE IN MY LIFE. I AM NOT CONCERNED WITH GOSSIP OR BEING GOSSIPED ABOUT.

THANK YOU, FATHER, FOR REMINDING ME THAT I HAVE BETTER THINGS TO DO THAN GOSSIP. I TURN MY

ENERGY TO CREATIVE ACHIEVEMENT AND LEAVE GOSSIP ALONE.

I THINK BEFORE I SPEAK. I AM CAREFUL WITH MY WORDS. I DO NOT MEDDLE OR PRY INTO SOMETHING THAT IS NONE OF MY BUSINESS. I USE MY ENERGY FOR GOOD.

□ *GREED* □

Those who are greedy are basically insecure: they amass fortunes, covet the possessions of others, collect prestige and material goods—all because they fear the unknown and hope that by the accumulation of tangible goods, they will arm themselves against monsters who inhabit the fearsome dark. Or, they frantically seek fame and power, thinking that when these are ensnared, all doubts will vanish and they will no longer feel anxious and unloved.

Benedict de Spinoza speaks of greed: "Avarice, ambition, lust . . . are nothing but species of madness, although not enumerated among diseases." Rid yourself of this energy-robbing greed. Overcome your avarice and covetousness. This craving for more and more only snowballs, and thus you are never satisfied with what you have, and you may miss something better in your mad dash of mindless lust. The poet Zeno wrote that "The avaricious man is like the barren sandy ground of the desert which sucks in all the rain and dew with greediness, but yields no fruitful herbs or plants for the benefit of others."

Use Red color energy to gain control of your greed. Red gives great personal power in times like these, and greed is a tacky little emotion that requires a surprising amount of energy to get rid of. The force of Red will allow you to turn your back on avarice and greed, and look instead to reasonable, rational, nondestructive horizons. After concentrating and absorbing Red's energy, seek balance and harmony with Green. Involve yourself in some activity in which you will not be tempted by greed, and wear a bright Red vest while you are doing it. Braid a bright, happy Red rag rug while you contemplate the abundance you already possess, then turn your thoughts to enjoying that abundance.

THANK YOU, FATHER, FOR MY ABUNDANT HEALTH AND WEALTH. I HAVE MORE THAN ENOUGH—FAR MORE THAN I COULD EVER DESIRE OR PRAY FOR.

I OVERCOME GREED. I TURN MY BACK ON GRASPING, CRAVING, LUSTING BEHAVIOR. I HOLD MY HEAD HIGH BECAUSE I AM PROUD OF WHO I AM AND WHAT I HAVE.

I SLASH THIS CANCEROUS GREED FROM MY MIND. I HEAL THE WOUND WITH LOVE AND APPRECIATION.

□ *GUILT* □

Guilt is the antithesis of love and the enemy of joy. Guilt is a harmful emotion which preys on peace of mind and health. Guilt is an emotion that accomplishes terrible pain; it sits like a lump of ice in the heart. To rid life of crippling guilt, you must take action.

Begin by forgiving yourself, and if it is possible, seek forgiveness from those you have wronged. After that, take action to put guilt behind you. Since we continue to live and breathe, then we continue to sin and make mistakes. It is not reasonable to carry around a load of guilt throughout life, piling guilt upon guilt until we finally grind to a stop and die. Guilt is a form of self-flagellation: if you keep hurling accusations at yourself, and moan and punish yourself, you will never become whole and healthy again. Guilt is a spiritual warning signal that alerts us to a spiritual malfunction—something is out of balance—and the problem yearns to be resolved.

If the mind cannot forgive or seek forgiveness, the mind passes its pain around, first to the spirit, then the body. Guilt, like prejudice, is a cancer.

Orange, the energy of hope, can help resolve guilt. In the midst of gloomy, dark guilt, Orange rays remind us that tomorrow will come with new opportunities. Orange reminds us that we can grow and mature, that forgiveness works, that guilt is a morass of emotional trauma we can do without. This energy snaps us into action, for action will help cure guilt.

I ACKNOWLEDGE MY MISDOINGS AND I AM FORGIVEN. I LAY DOWN MY BURDEN OF GUILT. I DO NOT PLACE BLAME.

I STEP OUT OF THE QUICKSAND OF GUILT AND ONTO THE FIRM GROUND OF HAPPINESS. THANK YOU, FATHER, FOR ABSOLUTION AND FORGIVENESS.

I TURN TOWARD THE LIGHT. I AM CLEANSED AND RENEWED. THANK YOU, FATHER, FOR ANOTHER MOMENT IN WHICH TO LIVE FULLY AND FREELY.

□ *HATRED* □

Byron wrote that "Hatred is the madness of the heart." It is an all-consuming fire which destroys everything in its path. Nothing can flourish—nay, nothing can live at all—where hatred is. What love builds, hatred tears down. It is a self-inflicted punishment more awful than the torture of the damned. It is frightening to know, also, that hate is a boomerang which will eventually circle back to slap us in the face.

Hate is like gangrene, with its baggage of vindictiveness, revenge, dishonor, and jealousy. It grows and grows, eating healthy flesh, and finally consumes us and we die, maybe not physically but surely in the heart and mind. A heart ruled by hate is not a heart at all; it is a shriveled dark thing where no light of life shines. Hate can flourish only where love is absent.

Hatred is an emotion which requires the use of all man's faculties—all the energy available in the universe. The first step in conquering hatred should begin with Red color energy. Red cauterizes the wound of hatred. It purifies by fire this terrible emotion. A blast of Red rays, focused on the festering sore of hatred on the soul, enables man to get past that first tough barrier. Red powers the mind to spurn hatred with its creeping slime of destructive emotions and to deal harshly with it.

To overcome hatred, a strong power must be called upon. To energize ourselves to combat hatred in any form, light a Red candle. Red will conquer; Red will vanquish this destructive force. Red provides a singing war cry as we banish hatred from our lives. We recommend that the battle with the hatred in your soul begin with candles in a quiet place when all your energy can be focused at once.

I CALL FOR YOU, FATHER, TO AID ME IN BANISHING HATRED FROM MY LIFE!

I SAY NO. I DO NOT HATE. HATE HAS NO PLACE IN MY LIFE. I CONTROL WHAT HAPPENS TO ME AND WHAT I FEEL. HATRED IS NOT AMONG THE INVITED GUESTS AT MY LIFE PARTY. GET THEE OUT OF MY LIFE, O HATEFUL THING.

HATRED IS ALL BUT A SCARY MEMORY NOW. GONE. GONE.

THANK YOU, FATHER, FOR THE ASSURANCE THAT LOVE TRIUMPHS OVER HATRED. I LOVE, I FEEL, I REACH OUT—GENTLE LOVE SOOTHES ME AND MAKES ME WELL.

□ *LONELINESS* □

First, get to know yourself and like yourself well enough when you are alone. This can be a wonderfully beneficial time: you can stretch your imagination, study about problems, make plans, relax, or accomplish tasks you couldn't while you are with others. When you put your time alone to good use, aloneness is not something to be avoided, it is something to be deliberately scheduled!

Lonely people are those who do not think they are complete or happy unless they have an abundance of companionship; they feel remote and isolated unless other people are milling around them. Lonely people don't like themselves very much and are frightened at what they might find in their own minds if they were ever alone. Lonely people sometimes form bad habits like initiating destructive relationships, taking on evasive bad habits, running away from problems and placing blame elsewhere, or even shaming themselves. They think, If I were less boring, more likable, less shy . . . I wouldn't feel lonely. These people do, of course, possess the resources inside them to feel fine when they are alone. The resources are just buried beneath some incorrect data.

Know that you are loved even if you happen to be alone. Know that you still have deep recesses of imagination and intelligence inside you that haven't been discovered yet. Know that an inner voyage of discovery can be the most satisfying trip you ever take.

After you are comfortable with who you are, you can plan to be alone some of the time; it is even necessary for the rejuvenation of our souls. Orange color energy helps the lonely one. It points out positive features about the lonely personality. It yearns to laugh, be merry, to love and be loved. Orange energy is friendly, for we must be friends with ourselves to be happy. These rays strum the heart-strings, producing a tiny smile at the corners of the mouth. Use Orange to jolt yourself out of the doldrums!

MY ALONE TIME IS PRECIOUS TO ME. I AM NEVER LONELY—THANK YOU, FATHER.

I PLAN MY ALONE TIME TO RENEW MYSELF, AND I CHERISH THESE QUIET TIMES.

LONELINESS EVAPORATES. EVEN WHEN I AM ALONE, I AM NOT LONELY.

□ *LOSS, GRIEF, AND DEATH* □

Life is filled with transition and change, and emotional pain is a reality. Whether the pain comes from a traumatic change, career crisis, broken relationship, or loss of a loved one through death, people will feel loss and will grieve. Most people view grief with fear, and they abhor it as a purely negative aspect of existence. In truth, grieving is healing, and this emotional pain is a very human way of demanding change or adjustment to change.

Normal grief is intense in its onset but it weakens with time. Soon it becomes a memory and holds no power over us. But those who cling to grief and loss too long doom themselves to emotional ruin. Some people even nourish their grief, and they wallow around in it . . . because it is known, something familiar, something they can tag and file in the emotional files of the mind. Holding on to pain consumes vast quantities of energy; it destroys creativity; it weighs us down and exhausts us. Fully functional people know that grief and loss will be a part of life, and that they are an integral part of growth. Emotional pain is real and cannot be denied; it will have its day.

Blue energy allows us to learn from loss, grief, and death. It offers an energy which transcends suspicion, callousness, and skepticism. Soothing Blue rays point out that we need not punish ourselves needlessly or too long, and that this facet of life must be endured. We can never predict when loss, grief, or death will come to us, so we are never fully prepared. The first step in dealing with this impermanent feeling is to accept it. Let the pain wash over you—if you resist it, you give it power. After your ordeal by fire—grieving—you may begin to heal yourself and grow emotionally stronger from the condition.

Blue allows us to understand that death and loss are simply aspects of the life cycle. Through this acceptance, Blue rays emit an energy which allows us to appreciate and value each encounter with loss, grief, and death.

I HAVE GREAT INNER STRENGTH. I GRIEVE APPROPRIATELY AND IT HURTS. MY SORROW IS DEEP AND MEANINGFUL.

THANK YOU, FATHER, FOR THE STRENGTH TO FEEL PAIN BUT NOT DRIFT INTO DESPAIR. THANK YOU FOR HOPE, FATHER, THE ANCHOR OF MY LIFE AND THE LIGHT OF THE FUTURE.

EVERY DAY I AM FILLED WITH HEALING ENERGY. I ACCEPT, I ENDURE, I GROW.

□ *MEMORY AND FORGETFULNESS* □

A faulty memory is a real confidence sapper. We feel vulnerable and stupid if we forget something, especially if it is an insignificant detail. It is very embarrassing when we forget some important fact; it is an assault on the image we hold of ourselves as whole and capable. Forgetfulness, some think, reflects poorly on the ability and competence of the mind.

Memory lapses, however, are not unusual and they are

not big red warning flags that senility is closing in. Eighty percent of those who live to ripe old age suffer no memory loss or very little. It is simply that the focus of the mind changes and we become concerned with different things as we grow older. And a good memory is not something you "have," but a process of the mind.

When the mind remembers information, it has been stored away, cross-referenced, and called up from some library in the brain. If forgetfulness is a problem, then make more cross-references and associate more related facts. Then the information is more accessible. The ability to remember something depends on two questions: did you put it into memory and is it accessible? When you commit information to memory, consciously place it in the brain library and consciously make a mental note as to where it has been stored.

A good memory can be cultivated, and Indigo color energy intensifies the cultivation process. Since Indigo is directly connected to any function of the mind, these rays can enhance the memory ability. A tried-and-true method one college professor uses is to write down, in Indigo-colored ink, the fact he wants to remember on a small white card. Just the idea that he has gone to the trouble of assembling the tools with which to write it makes its accessibility immediately available. Indigo vibrations help release the mind's hidden knowledge, and we are able to recall information stored there.

Indigo energizes the mind's capacity to perform somewhat like a computer, with lightning-fast focus, to illumine. Indigo also relaxes the physical body and turns the energy toward the mind. Relax, turn on your Indigo-powered mind computer and recall that fact, remember that name, summon those figures!

MY MIND IS RAZOR-SHARP. ANY INFORMATION I WISH IS IMMEDIATELY AVAILABLE TO ME. MY ATTENTION

SCROLLS THROUGH THE NEATLY ORDERED LIBRARY OF MY MEMORY.

THANK YOU, FATHER, FOR THIS FANTASTIC BRAIN! MY RECALL IS ASTOUNDING! MEMORIES APPEAR EFFORTLESSLY UPON THE SCREEN IN MY HEAD.

I SUMMON DESIRED INFORMATION IN THE SNAP OF THE FINGER! ASK ME ANYTHING! I'LL REMEMBER!

□ *OVERCOMING JEALOUSY* □

Human beings have trouble defining the meaning of jealousy, but it is a desperate barrage of emotions that threatens to sweep reality away forever. While a feeling of jealousy is sometimes normal, the behavior it elicits is irrational and destructive. Overwhelming jealousy is a signal that self-esteem is reaching a low point and that insecurity has shifted into road gear.

Jealousy and possessiveness are one; many times possessiveness is the kiss of death to a romantic relationship. Nobody enjoys feeling smothered and/or controlled, limited or dictated to, especially the participants in a delicate, emotional romance. Possessiveness is detrimental to both parties: the possessor worries constantly that the partner will drift away unless stringent measures are taken to recapture the prey; the possessee squirms under the watchful eye of the ringmaster and soon begins to seek relief and freedom.

Jealousy is one response human beings feel when they sense the danger of losing something they love. Usually manifested in connection with a loving relationship, jealousy is unreasonable and irrational if the relationship is secure and stable. Those participants in a truly loving and trusting relationship do not fear betrayal and do not experience jealousy.

Jealousy is a monster. It consumes and dirties everything in its path—it wrecks relationships, soils trust, and allows fear to spread rampantly through life. Overcome jealousy and you do away with a giant area of fear in a relationship. Do you really think you have so little to give when compared with your partner? Are you really so lacking in self-esteem that you jealously guard your love, shielding it from growth-providing light and air? Do you want to shut off the life-giving light and the nurturing openness life provides, thereby squelching growth and health? Jealousy is the elephant doo-doo in the circus parade of life—sidestep it.

Allow love to flourish. Expose it to the light and air; encourage your love to seek new heights and new strengths! It can only bring you joy as you gain deeper understanding in each other. Illuminate the dark corners of your jealous mind with Yellow rays. Seek and destroy that muckraking jealousy and replace it with trust, dignity, and freedom. Jealousy dries up, crusts over, and flakes away when it is exposed to healthy, happy Yellow color energy.

When you feel a hint of jealousy, immediately surround yourself with Yellow color energy, then proceed with self-examination. What prompted the jealous feeling? Is it a response to your own lack of self-worth? Put on a bright Yellow T-shirt that shouts "I love my life; I love my lover; I trust my loving relationship; and I exhibit dignity, happiness, and self-esteem."

JEALOUSY HAS NO PLACE IN MY LOVING RELATIONSHIP. I DO NOT FEAR—I DO NOT GIVE ENERGY TO SO DESTRUCTIVE AN EMOTION.

I TRUST, I LOVE, I LIVE—CLEANLY AND JOYOUSLY. I AM A WORTHY PERSON, NOT DISTRACTED WITH PITIFUL JEALOUSY. I RISE ABOVE IT!

THANK YOU, FATHER, FOR THE RATIONAL, REASONABLE, SOUND, SECURE, LOVING RELATIONSHIP I TEND WITH THE GREATEST CARE. THANK YOU FOR THE CAPACITY TO BANISH FEAR AND JEALOUSY FROM MY LIFE.

□ *PATIENCE* □

Although the dictionary states that patience is the power or capacity to endure without complaint something difficult or disagreeable, we add to that the ability to wait calmly, without anxiety. Today's world society has no patience; we hurry up and thrash around, spewing energy spasmodically, gnashing our teeth because we are impatient. We seem to visibly disintegrate when we must wait for something to happen, somebody else to do something or make a decision, or in a thousand other situations which call for us to sit quietly for a time.

We'd be so much better off if we'd acquire a little patience. To be able to sit with composure, coolly, is an attribute we could all use. Sometimes it is just inevitable that we must wait or endure. It behooves us to learn patience.

Blue, of course, is for patience. Its spiritual softness gentles human beings and lengthens bunched-up nerves and muscles. Blue energy helps us remain serene. Cultivate tolerance and patience in Blue's gentle rays.

If you are required to wait, for any purpose, think before you get to the waiting place: take along a book or a notepad and make lists, or tackle some problem which requires thought during the waiting time. Use the time-energy fruitfully, to some purpose. Blue makes waiting easier, and fosters patience in the Father's antsy children.

I TAKE DEEP SLOW BREATHS; MY MUSCLES AND NERVES RELAX. I AM PATIENT, CALM, AND COOL.

THANK YOU, FATHER, FOR THIS BREATHER. I AM FILLED WITH FORBEARANCE, TOLERANCE, AND SELF-CONTROL.

MY FIRST REACTION TO STRESS IS CALM STRENGTH. FILL ME NOW, GENTLE PATIENCE, WITH THE STRENGTH TO LAST.

□ *PREJUDICE* □

Prejudice is demonstrated by holding an emphatic opinion without good reason. What a mild definition of a terrible state! Prejudice is a cancer eating away at the soul of mankind. Nothing, *nothing*, good ever comes from being prejudiced against someone else without good reason. And, sorrowfully, every human being feels prejudice in some degree. Get ready to be made uncomfortable.

Here are some prejudices: fat people, handicapped people, beautiful people, redheads, poor people, racial and ethnic groups, thin people, smart people, commoners, the aristocracy, mentally retarded people, blind people, deaf people, cowboys, cops, short people, tall people, people not of the same religion, atheists, lawyers, midwives . . .

Let's stop here. Suffice it to say that prejudice is destructive and we all feel it sometimes. The fear of the unfamiliar coupled with a feeling of vulnerability makes a bubbling stew of prejudice within us. Let's stop prejudice or at least recognize it and deal with it, then put it away.

Orange energy overcomes prejudice. Like a puppy, Orange rays illuminate us and make us friendly—and show that friendliness makes friends. One man told his former wife, "I don't want our son having Mexican friends; you'll just have to put your foot down." What a petty little man. What a narrow, underdeveloped mind.

If you feel an illogical prejudice trying to slip into your mind, whip it out immediately and examine it for flaws. If it has no "bottom" or has a false bottom (lack of truth), then squeeze it out.

Orange is the color for the banishment of prejudice. This energy is just too positive to tolerate bias or one-sidedness. Orange rays light up the positive virtues. Orange is aware; it brings truth to the forefront of the mind and imagination.

I HOLD INFORMED JUDGMENTS BASED ON FAIR EVALUATIONS. I SEEK TRUTH AND VIRTUE IN MYSELF AND IN OTHERS. I DO NOT BUY INTO GROUNDLESS FEARS, BIASED OR SLANTED OPINIONS, OR HURTFUL, HATEFUL PRINCIPLES.

THANK YOU, FATHER, FOR THE ABILITY TO JUDGE MYSELF AND OTHERS IN THE LIGHT OF TRUTH AND HONESTY. THANK YOU FOR THE MATURITY TO SEE CLEARLY.

□ *REGRETS AND REMORSE* □

Because we are human, we will make mistakes. We will want to slap ourselves for making an unthinking remark. We'll cringe in embarrassment when we think of the hurtful act we performed. We'll be sad and sorrowful about some foolish outburst that caused another pain.

And then it is necessary for us to feel remorseful and regretful. That state of mind can be blown all out of proportion. If you keep flogging yourself for some sin you've committed, way past time to give it up and move on, your life begins to smell like rotted fish. The odor of decay will filter into all the rooms of your mind and color every thought and action. If you feel sorry for something you've done or said, or omitted doing or saying, admit it. Acknowledge it, forgive and climb out of the vat of remorse. If you are sorry, say, "I am heartily sorry for saying this or doing that." Then let yourself off the hook.

What you'll feel is incredible relief. Don't brood; take

action. Orange energy helps us get by these terrible times of remorse. Orange gives us hope for a better day, one in which we make fewer mistakes, learn gentleness toward ourselves, which causes us to feel gentler toward others. Orange is the ray of positive human qualities: it acknowledges that we make mistakes and it points the way to forgiveness.

Some people have the colossal nerve to brag about never having apologized. These people are sick and deserve no merit badge of achievement. Steer clear of anyone who brags that he's never apologized for anything in his life—underneath whatever exterior he sports, decay has riddled the inner man. (This man probably wouldn't be caught dead wearing an Orange shirt!)

I ERRED. I MADE A MISTAKE. I GRIEVE FOR MY FOOLISHNESS.

MY ACT OF CONTRITION IS THE APOLOGY I MAKE WITH PURE PENITENCE.

I FORGIVE. I FORGIVE MYSELF.

THANK YOU, FATHER, FOR THE SOLACE AVAILABLE TO ME. THANK YOU, FATHER, FOR FORGIVENESS. MY MISTAKE FALLS AWAY; MY ERROR IS ENDED.

I MOVE FORWARD FREELY, WISER AND MORE MATURE.

□ *SHAME, DISHONOR, DISGRACE* □

Aren't you just a little presumptuous when you feel ashamed? The Father lost His Son so that you would never have to feel shame. Would you belittle that supreme sacrifice? Would you preempt the Father's judgment with your own?

We've all done things we wished we hadn't, and we've all made mistakes. But if we brood on it and dwell on disgrace, we mire ourselves in the swamp of shame and we never get over it. Handle dishonor or errors in judgment realistically. Admit, atone if need be, and get over it. Decide not to perform that behavior in the future. Realize your ineptitude or your foot-in-mouth disease and resolve to be more careful from now on.

If you commit some act that leaves you feeling diminished in stature in your own eyes, or if you say something that hurts someone else and feel sorry, by all means take action to leave that situation behind. First, acknowledge your mistake, seek forgiveness from yourself and from the person you wronged, and then just get over it.

The person of low self-esteem has a poor reputation with himself. The person of high self-esteem realizes that even if he commits some transgression, at least he is moving and shaking, attempting to grow and learn. If you are scared to death to make a mistake, you give energy to that fear—then look for yourself to make a lot of mistakes in the future; you've just alerted your mind to develop that picture.

Seek balance. Remember the good things you do and the good things you can do in the future. Then do some of those good things. Smite your forehead in frustration and apologize sincerely. Promise to do better from now on. Hurry to right that wrong. Present the one you wronged with a bouquet of Yellow wildflowers you spontaneously pick from a meadow. Say, "I'm so sorry; I regret that I hurt you. I'll try never to do it again."

In the quiet, while you are alone, honestly look at the behavior, acknowledge it, acknowledge your transgression, and make a firm commitment to avoid that behavior in the future. Gaze solemnly into the stalwart flame from your Yellow candle and say this:

I DID SOMETHING AWFUL BUT I AM NOT AN AWFUL PERSON. I TAKE ALL ACTIONS TO MINIMIZE MY MISTAKE AND ATONE.

NOW I MOVE ON. I SHAKE THIS OFF AND I REMEMBER THAT MY SIN IS ULTIMATELY PAID FOR. THANK YOU, FATHER.

I MAKE THIS FIRM VERBAL COMMITMENT. I WILL NOT BEHAVE IN THE FUTURE AS I HAVE BEHAVED IN THE PAST. I THROW THAT BEHAVIOR IN THE SHINY SILVER TRASH CAN OF LIFE AND FIRMLY ATTACH THE LID.

□ *SORROW* □

The emotions of joy and sorrow are sacred and divine, but the excess of either is destructive. A natural sadness or grief helps the body and mind get past some sorrowful event. But those who dwell on sorrow, those who languish in its smothering arms, deprive themselves of precious time and energy. Poet Albert Smith believed that "Tears are the safety valve of the heart when too much pressure is laid on it." Tears are cleansing, and appropriate sorrow is necessary. To sorrow is human, but this feeling is never fixed: it is a transitory emotion which allows us to respectfully feel sad for another or for ourselves. Heartache, misery, and distress are all facets of sorrow.

If you have suffered a loss or grieve for something or someone, you are entitled to do so. Be aware that during your sorrowful time, tension is building inside you and it will eventually demand some release. Be gentle with yourself, however, and float quietly on the soft energy of the universe. Use soothing color energy for this emotion. At the appropriate time, seek life and normality again.

Use Red color energy to pull yourself up from the depths of sadness. Anytime human beings need to climb out of a deep emotion, Red rays will provide the energy. Red is a happy, invigorating color, and if the sorrowing one will allow it to work its power, getting back into normal life will be a simple, gradual transition. Red's energizing rays will brighten the spirits, stir enthusiasm, and rekindle the lust for life at its most enjoyable.

In order to put sorrow away and get past the painful event or circumstance, light a sparkling Red candle, repaint the doghouse with bright Red paint, construct a birdhouse and paint it Red, put up some inexpensive posters splashed with fun, exciting Red, and say:

I LEARN FROM MY SORROW, FATHER. IN THE ARMS OF SORROW, I FEEL PAIN AND LOSS. I GRIEVE APPROPRIATELY.

THANK YOU, FATHER, FOR THE STRENGTH TO TRIUMPH OVER SORROW—TO HEAL THIS CLEAN WOUND AND MOVE FORWARD.

I DO NOT WHINE AND I DO NOT WALLOW IN SELF-PITY. I SORROW APPROPRIATELY AND I RISE AGAIN TO FACE THE LIGHT.

□ *SUSPICION AND INSECURITY* □

Suspicion is the manifestation of insecurity and lack of trust. Sometimes we hear people described as having a suspicious nature, meaning that they never trust anyone and are always looking for some betrayal. No one can teach you to become secure and less suspicious except yourself.

These two demons erode self-confidence and project energy outward into the void, with no hope of a return on the investment. If we take our self-image from how we are affected by others, we're betting on the outcome. This is a mistake. How much better to get to know yourself and know you can depend on you always. Why do you need to search out possible betrayals if you are whole and healthy yourself? If you channel enough energy into hunting betrayals, look for it to happen in your life. If you expect a child to cheat and you communicate that thought, he might just satisfy it; if you continually suspect your lover of dallying with somebody else, he might just get the message that that is what you expect to happen and want to happen. Horrors!

People who are insecure do not know themselves and they do not believe in themselves or their abilities. Joan was the clarion horn of suspicion. You could always count on Joan to voice suspicion, to be the naysayer, to warn against trusting. Joan lived a shallow, barren existence, unadorned with joy or confidence. She spent so much time guarding against bad things that she allowed her positive attributes to wither on the vine.

Orange energy lessens suspicion and offers security. Orange, this extroverted joyous color, banishes suspicion because it encourages insecure ones to find their own positive attributes. It concentrates on the good points of others' personalities, and knows that it is not necessary to completely buy into another's personality, but to enjoy his or her good traits.

Orange allows you to find the good points in yourself and to trust your own actions and reactions. Orange rays promote a sense that each of us is needed, wanted, and loved.

I HAVE NO TIME FOR SUSPICIONS. I HAVE NO ENERGY TO SPARE FOR INSECURITIES. I LOOK FOR POSITIVE CHARACTERISTICS IN MYSELF AND IN OTHERS.

THANK YOU, FATHER, FOR I AM AN END IN MYSELF. I POSSESS ALL THE ENERGY I'LL EVER NEED.

I POOH-POOH SUSPICION AND DEPEND ON MY OWN GOOD ACTIONS, THOUGHTS, AND DEEDS.

□ *TOLERANCE* □

There is a short supply of tolerance these days. We are impatient, contemptuous, and disgusted. We think *our* way is the best way, and that *our* opinions matter more than the opinion of any other. Consequently, we make life more difficult and frustrating than it has to be.

The Father created us differently. We all hold different opinions and formulate individual methods for information-accumulating and problem-solving. Our methods are not necessarily more effective or more important than someone else's, and we might be able to learn something from someone else if we pay attention. Tolerance is possible and achievable; we just have to teach ourselves to display it.

The energy emanated by Gold furthers our struggle toward tolerance. It supports us in the belief that all human beings matter and that the opinions and thoughts of those other human beings might just be as valuable as our own. Gold says "lighten up" and "slow down" and "stop and think a moment." It aids in making us willing to put up with the beliefs and actions of which we do not approve, and allows others to think and do as they see fit.

Find a painting, photograph, or picture from a magazine depicting someone exhibiting great tolerance. Read a book about great statesmen and arbitrators. Mentally remind yourself to be tolerant of the beliefs of others, and contemplate the warm energy of Gold.

THANK YOU, FATHER, FOR I AM TOLERANT AND PATIENT. MY OPINIONS ARE IMPORTANT, BUT SO ARE THE OPINIONS OF OTHERS.

I DO NOT NECESSARILY RUN MY LIFE ACCORDING TO THE METHODS OF OTHERS, BUT I RECOGNIZE THE VALUE OF DIFFERING METHODS. I ACCEPT THE FACT THAT OTHER HUMAN BEINGS LIVE ON THIS PLANET, AND ALL ARE VALUABLE.

THANK YOU, FATHER, FOR I PAUSE . . . I LISTEN . . . I HEAR. I LIVE WITH TOLERANCE TOWARD MY FELLOWMAN.

□ *WORRY AND ANXIETY* □

Ever had an anxiety attack? This physical manifestation of inner conflict takes many forms: sweaty palms, wide staring eyes, jittery nerves, and the list goes on. Human beings spend a large amount of time trying to avoid anxiety. What if this energy could be used to creatively change our lives?

Anxiety is an emotion and it can have great effect upon the physical organism. Anxiety symptoms can even develop into a real illness if they are not curtailed.

A person may not always be able to pinpoint the exact cause of his anxiety, but somewhere in his psyche lurks the worry/fear which is causing his anxiety. This emotional disturbance is sometimes preferable to a physical trauma like surgery or hospitalization. We'd rather undergo some painful physical treatment than face the murky fear in our mind! Amazing.

Anxiety is really an anticipatory fear: we anticipate the occurrence of a terrible event, or we dread a threatening stimulus which may or may not occur—usually not. Stress or pressure is the result of worry and anxiety. Some stress or pressure is beneficial to life, and the way to tell if stress is beneficial or destructive is to gauge how we react to it. If we faint and drop to the ground in a clump or if we fall apart, we have not reacted well to stress. Words that depict the healthy reaction to stress are cope and adapt. These words even apply to the top two stressful events of life: death of a spouse and divorce.

The solution to the stress-anxiety-worry-pressure dilemma is to go on experiencing life, minimizing the amount of negative stress on a day-to-day basis, and learning how to cope with it when it occurs. The body's response to stress is a nonspecific group: backaches, headaches, chronic fatigue, and depression are a few. In fact, worry and anxiety may even contribute to death. It drains vitality and can even affect the will to go on living.

If we were sensible all the time, we'd know automatically that worry is senseless. Worry erupts when we hold a mental picture of exactly what we *don't* want to happen. Consequently, anything we visualize, we give energy to, and (here comes the old refrain) the mind seeks to develop that picture.

Good old Indigo comes to the rescue. This energy makes it difficult for us to dwell on negative thoughts and makes it easier for us to replace those thoughts with positive ones. Indigo dissolves worry and anxiety. These fine, spiritual rays float those thoughts away and remind us that we can handle anything that comes along, any situation.

Deep, satisfying Indigo brings the depth, texture, and richness of life to mind. It energizes the higher aspects of enlightenment and illumines the wonderful qualities of being human. Indigo states boldly, "You cannot flee from what you still hold in your mind." Indigo helps replace the bad thoughts with good, healthy thoughts. You must direct this energy and allow it to work on uplifting the spirits, brightening the outlook, and pointing out the spiritual benefits of positive living.

STRESS AND PRESSURE DON'T GET ME DOWN. ANXIETY AND WORRY ARE FEARS I MANUFACTURED MYSELF.

SHOO, NEGATIVE THOUGHTS! GET AWAY, ANXIETY ATTACK! I AM IN CONTROL HERE, AND I DECLARE THAT PEACE SHALL REIGN.

I DON'T HUNT BOOGER-BEARS AND I DO NOT ATTRACT PROBLEMS. I TAKE LIFE AS IT COMES.

THANK YOU, FATHER, FOR YOU AND I TOGETHER CAN HANDLE ANY SITUATION. I HAVE ACCESS TO YOUR UNFAILING PROTECTION, AND WORRY HAS NO PLACE IN MY FUTURE.

C H A P T E R IX

PHYSICAL HEALTH

□ *ASTHMA* □

Possibly one of the most frightening health problems is asthma. The inability to breathe terrifies all of us, especially the asthmatic. This disease manifests itself when a person with asthma is exposed to an allergen. The circular muscles surrounding the smaller bronchial tubes spasm and reduce the airway so that little oxygen can go in or out. All this happens while the poor sufferer is awake, conscious of his air tubes growing smaller and smaller! Panic takes over to tense up the muscles even more. If immediate action is not taken, serious consequences can occur.

A physician must monitor the asthma-sufferer's condition. If you are diagnosed with asthma, be alert to your condition. Don't lapse into hypochondria, but be reasonably aware of what's going on with your body. There are ways you can help yourself and your treating physician to care for your body.

Medical science tells us that an asthma attack can be severely worsened if the person panics: muscles constrict with tension, frantic and impulsive movements draw energy away from the lungs, and the mind is chaotic—unable to help the body relax and breathe. Fear shuts down the thinking processes and complicates healing. The body does not like to endure an asthma attack, and subliminally the body is trying to get over it. If you panic and release a spurt of adrenaline in order to flap your arms and legs, less energy is available for your lungs.

See a doctor and follow his advice. After an asthma attack has ceased and your body is relaxing, picture yourself as giving some of the energy you expended back to the universe. As you breathe in, picture soft Orange air full of light and warmth. Let that light and warmth flow through you. As you breathe out, send light and warmth back into the cosmos. Send your happy and grateful Orange air into the universe, to come to the aid of others.

Orange tells us to hope. Orange light warms us and relaxes us; it tells us to use the limitless positive energy of the world to heal ourselves. Within the human mind and body is a great self-healing force. Orange energy illumines this ability.

SLOWLY I BREATHE IN THE SOFT, WARM AIR OF THE UNIVERSE. THANK YOU, FATHER.

SLOWLY I BREATHE OUT. I REPLACE THE AIR GIVEN TO ME WITH LIGHT AND WARMTH FROM MY BODY. THANK YOU, FATHER.

I RELAX MY BODY. I AM GENTLE WITH MY BODY AND MY BODY GROWS STRONG. I CONTROL FEAR AND PANIC—THESE HAVE NO PLACE HERE.

I SLOW THE PACE.

□ *BRONCHITIS AND COUGHS* □

As awful as it seems, the cough is nature's way of clearing air passages. The entire respiratory system benefits from coughing: secretions are cleared from the throat, lungs, and larynx. A chronic or intermittent cough can be a symptom of bronchitis, an infection or inflammation of the bronchial tubes. Bronchitis will slip up on you, so be alert to your body's warning signals: a persistent cough needs to be evaluated by a physician.

When you have a disease of the respiratory region of the body, a cough is most likely going to occur. How can you make this symptom less uncomfortable? Don't breathe cold air, drink soothing warm liquids—herbal teas are good—rest, relax, and generally be good to your body. Surround yourself with positive, uplifting colors and create an atmosphere of healing. Orange is a wonderful self-healing encourager.

Light an Orange candle and let its cheery light lift your spirits and make your convalescence easier to deal with. Orange juice is full of healing elements, providing vitamin C and other nutrients. Since a cold usually accompanies a cough, use Orange in your room to brighten and warm the atmosphere. Be nice to yourself.

I MOVE IN SYNCHRONIZATION WITH MY BODY'S RHYTHMS TO PROMOTE HEALING.

THANK YOU, FATHER, FOR THE WARMTH AND LIGHT AVAILABLE TO MY VALUABLE BODY. THANK YOU FOR REST AND HEALING.

I AM WORTHY OF GOOD CARE. I TAKE GOOD CARE OF MYSELF. I GATHER MY ENERGIES TO COMBAT ILLNESS. PURE LIGHT COURSES THROUGH MY VEINS.

□ *THE COMMON COLD* □

"By 'ead 'urts. By dose is runny. I feel reeeaaalllly bad."

That is what the common cold may do to human beings, and since colds are caused by viruses, there is no known cure. Cold remedies provide short-term relief for some symptoms, but nothing will get you over a cold except the passage of about seven days.

Many home remedies are just as useful (and substantially cheaper) than over-the-counter medicines. Herbal tea flavored with honey and lemon soothes aches caused by colds, as does breathing a concoction of eucalyptus leaves in boiling water. You just can't do much for a cold, so any remedy that offers some respite from that draggy, ouchful feeling caused by a cold is good to try.

Blow your nose on a bright Red hanky and lay your aching head on a Red pillow. Pull on your fuzzy Red socks and cover up with a warm Red blanket. Light your Red candle and hope that time fast-forwards to good health!

I FUNCTION DESPITE SMALL HINDRANCES. MY BUSY LIFE ALLOWS LITTLE ENERGY TO BE WASTED ON SMALL CONCERNS.

I BREATHE, I MOVE, I LIVE IN A GREAT ENERGY FIELD. I TAKE ENERGY FROM MY ENVIRONMENT AND USE IT TO ACCOMPLISH TASKS.

THANK YOU, FATHER, FOR MY RESILIENT NATURE, FOR MY WONDERFUL BODY, WHICH MAY BE SLOWED BY ILLNESS BUT NEVER STOPPED. THE LIGHT WITHIN ME BURNS STRONG AND SURE.

□ *DIARRHEA* □

We are not about to tell you that in order to get over diarrhea all you have to do is light a Green candle. Human beings seem to be preoccupied with this type of body function, and we seem to think it is amusing to mention. However, there is nothing funny about abdominal cramps or the non-availability of a bathroom when human beings suffer from diarrhea.

Most attacks of the trots are caused by viral infections, and some attacks are brought on by what we eat and drink. But sometimes we get diarrhea because we are upset and stressed. This may be the only manifestation of stress, but it is a doozy. In order to control nervous diarrhea, stress must be controlled. Ease your mind and the body will ease also.

In order to get ahold of stress and calm nervous diarrhea, use the healing, balancing energy of Green. When the mind, body, and spirit are harmonious—aligned—and functioning smoothly, the physical manifestations of inward stress depart. Green seeks to bring all aspects of life into complete accord. Since the basic premise of color therapy is to use certain energies to aid the human being, Green will work on all parts of the human condition, bringing powers together and focusing on the ideal state of existence.

When nervous diarrhea strikes, immediately shift gears: slow down, contemplate, take control, and utilize basic reasoning processes. Identify the problem and seek the root of the distress. Examine the problem and focus energy toward dealing with it. Surround yourself in healing Green energy—through nature or through whatever means are easily available—and strive for balance, regularity, harmony, and tranquillity.

I SLOW THE ACTION. I SINK BACK INTO A SOFT HAVEN OF SERENITY. I DIVE DEEP INTO MY CONSCIOUSNESS AND SEND MESSAGES TO MY PHYSICAL BODY: "BE EASY. GO SMOOTHLY."

THANK YOU, FATHER, FOR THE WHISPER-SOFT LESSENING OF MY BODY'S DISTRESS. I FIND THE SOURCE OF DISTRESS AND SEND IT AWAY. THANK YOU, FATHER, FOR MY SMOOTHLY FUNCTIONING BODY. THANK YOU FOR THE LACK OF PAIN. THANK YOU FOR PERFECT HEALTH.

□ *FATIGUE AND LOW ENERGY* □

Fatigue is one of those vague, indistinct maladies we wrestle with occasionally. Sometimes we just feel tired, and even a good night's rest doesn't energize us much. We slump around like we're dragging an anvil; we don't even have the energy to complain. Fatigue is somewhat like the Without Syndrome though nowhere near as debilitating. Fatigue and low energy can be overcome with a little bit of effort.

Sometimes we need a little rest-time so our bodies can rebuild energy reserves. Human beings are not robots and the body can't go at full steam all the time. If the body feels sluggish and energy-poor, it may be sending the mind a message. After you've analyzed the feeling of fatigue and recognized its purpose, you can still accomplish tasks which utilize a small amount of energy. Use Red color energy for inertia.

Search for activities that pique your interest. Find something nice to do for yourself. Spend some quiet time expending little energy, but accomplishing some satisfying task. Clean out your top desk drawer—you can do that sitting at your desk. Watch a movie while lying on the couch. Soak in a bubble bath. Take an inventory of what's in your fingernail care box. Count how many washers you see in your tool kit. It's okay. It really is. You get to do those things sometimes simply because you want to. And you are entitled to be comfortable while you do it.

Put on your Red sweat suit and your fluffy Red house slippers. Dress in your favorite Red flannel shirt, the one with the hole in the elbow. Red color energy will help in dealing with fatigue and low energy. It will inject a spark that might get you moving again.

To overcome fatigue and up those sluggish energy levels, use Red and bask in its invigorating rays.

I MARSHAL MY FORCES FOR ACTION. I TAKE THIS QUIET TIME TO REFLECT ON THE VAST WAREHOUSE OF ENERGY AVAILABLE INSIDE ME.

I CALL UPON MY LIMITLESS ENERGY TO MOVE BRISKLY, TO SET A GOAL, TO REACH AND COMPLETE MY GOAL.

THANK YOU, FATHER . . . I BEGIN TO FEEL THE ELECTRIC TINGLE OF ENERGY AS IT POPS AND EXPLODES AROUND ME. IT SEEPS INTO MY BEING NOW. I FEEL MYSELF GLOW AND PULSE WITH LIGHT.

□ *FEVER* □

Human beings function much like the heating and cooling systems of our homes and our automobiles, at least to the extent that we depend on a "thermostat." Our bodies have a thermostat built in, and the mind registers any significant increase or decrease in the normal temperature of the body. Running a fever or having a temperature is a signal that an infection is brewing somewhere in the body. It is indicative of some profound disturbance in the human machine.

Sometimes the body will feel flushed or hot with a fever, and sometimes the body shakes with chills. However the mechanism works, a fever should be immediately evaluated. Use common sense and beware of self-diagnosis and self-medicating. If you make a judgment that you probably need to see a doctor, then trot yourself to the phone and make an appointment. Don't drag around waiting for somebody to chastise your noble, self-denying stance. It is not reasonable to avoid getting the proper care for the precious vessel which contains your life. Use a little common sense.

A fever must run its course, and aided with the instructions from a health care professional, there are several things you can do to help your body get well. Orange color energy is good for fever in that it will lift your spirits. Don't immerse yourself in the color Orange though, because a person with fever should stay in bed and be quiet. Orange energy speeds recuperation. So, take your medicine, get in bed, and light your cheerful Orange candle.

I ACCEPT NOTHING BUT PERFECT HARMONY IN MY BODY AND MY MIND. I WORK WITH MY BODY'S DEFENSE MECHANISMS TO COMBAT INFECTION.

THANK YOU, FATHER, FOR MY SERENE STATE OF BEING, FOR MY GOOD COMMON SENSE, FOR MY WAREHOUSE OF BODILY STRENGTH.

WARM LIGHT CARESSES MY BODY AND GOOD HEALTH FLOWS THROUGH ME.

□ *HEADACHE* □

Having a headache is more of a nuisance than an illness. The man who has never endured a headache hasn't been born because headaches are as common as itching and are usually not life-threatening. This commonest of all human complaints sometimes heralds a real illness, so attention must be paid. But the vast majority of headaches are caused by stress and tension, and it is this type of head pain we address. Let us hasten to say that if you have a persistent, excruciating headache, see a health care professional; it may be a signal that something is organically out of kilter.

The treatment of a tension headache is strictly trial and error. Sometimes an aspirin will knock it, and sometimes no matter what we do, the headache lingers. No two headaches are exactly alike, but hope is available for the garden-variety headache.

To treat stress and tension, relaxation is the answer, and if stress and tension have manifested themselves by a dull, throbbing headache, seek relaxation. Take your shoes off, dim the lights, and close your eyes. Rest in a quiet place. Enter, via mind pictures if necessary, a lovely cool Blue environment. Pull on a soft Blue robe; wrap up in a cuddly Blue comforter. Light a soothing Blue candle. Relax and absorb Blue's spiritually calming rays.

Hopefully, if you treat a tension headache with Blue rays and a change in atmosphere, its duration will be brief and the intensity slight.

EYES—CLOSE SOFTLY. MUSCLES—RELAX. ARMS AND LEGS—BECOME FLOPPY AND EASY.

TENSION SEEPS AWAY FROM ME AND LEAVES ME IN PERFECT HEALTH. STRESS AND HEADACHE SLIP AWAY. I AM RELAXED AND SOOTHED.

THANK YOU, FATHER, FOR THIS REMINDER TO RELAX, FOR THIS SIGNPOST THAT SAYS "SLOW DOWN. BE EASY."

□ *HIGH BLOOD PRESSURE AND HYPERACTIVITY* □

Another way to describe high blood pressure is hypertension. The hyperactive person is one who is excessively or pathologically active. Hyperactive people tend to be hypertensive. Although this syndrome is a major medical concern, there is much we can do to aid health care professionals in the treatment of high blood pressure. Hypertension is not a disease in itself; it is a symptom of either an internal malfunction of the body or the body's poor response to external stress. It is interesting, however, that many patients diagnosed with hypertension fit the same mold: they are hard-driving, dynamic racehorses; they never have time to relax, are always in a rush, and are constantly in over their heads.

If your high blood pressure or hyperactivity is not medically related, then you probably exhibit one or more of the above-described characteristics. High blood pressure caused by external stress is just as physically dangerous as the internally caused hypertension. We won't recite the old cliché "Stop and smell the roses," but that phrase indicates the exact treatment.

Give yourself time to enjoy the journey toward a goal; savor the satisfaction of achieving a goal before you set another. Balance challenge with mastery. Move forward consistently, but take smaller steps. Realign priorities. Make room for happiness and recreation. The key word is balance and Green's energy epitomizes it.

Green soothes the harried worker, and it promotes a sense of ease, of nature's healing powers, and of a garden bower in which to relax and smell whatever flower happens to be there. Green equalizes pressure: you don't have to be the anxious executive-type to feel pressure; all people labor under some sort of pressure all the time. But you can alleviate pressure's detrimental capacity by taking reasonable actions and setting reasonable goals.

Green helps human beings adjust to the environment. It aids the hypertensive person to actually stop and recognize the beauty of the world and the power of the earth. Green promises harmony and balance, and reidentifies the individual power to regulate human environment. In essence, Green works on the heart and its functions by calming and strengthening. Concentration and deliberate slowing of the heart's action, coupled with the soothing use of Green rays, successfully lower blood pressure.

THE WORLD IS A LUSH GREEN PLANET, FULL OF LIFE AND NOURISHING ATTRIBUTES. I TAKE TIME TO PAUSE IN MY LIFE AND NOTICE THIS BEAUTY—I SLOW THE PACE. I RELAX.

I COME THANKING YOU AND PRAISING YOU, FATHER, FOR THE GIFT OF LIFE. I TAKE GOOD CARE OF THIS PRECIOUS VESSEL WHICH CONTAINS MY LIFE. MY BODY IS A FULLY FUNCTIONAL PERFECT ECHO OF YOUR CREATIVE IDEA.

□ *INDIGESTION* □

Together with indigestion, lumped into the same category, are several ailments: heartburn, bloat, sour stomach, and gas. Sometimes these symptoms indicate an organic disorder—a symptom of a malfunction or illness of the body. But garden-variety indigestion is probably caused by eating too much or eating too many spicy foods, causing gas or an abundance of stomach acids being manufactured. A tense person who exhibits poor eating habits and eats too much of the wrong kinds of food will surely have indigestion. Change your eating habits and you will experience greatly improved digestion: eat slowly, eat smaller meals, and avoid foods with a high fat content or foods that contain a lot of spice. Sometimes indigestion is caused by nervousness or stress. The Thwart Monster loves indigestion!

If you experience indigestion because of your life-style or the stress and tension you feel almost constantly, then rest assured that you can do something about it. When your body is very tense and your nerves are strung so tight that you can play "O, Susanna" on the cords of your neck, light a Yellow candle and calm your mind; adjust your mental thinking to affirm a healthy, serene atmosphere. Concentrate on your candle's flame and affirm your peace of mind, your competence to handle life's little upsets with confidence. Use Yellow's stimulating intellectual qualities to replace turmoil with tranquillity in your mind—your body will follow with a quiet, calm demeanor, and your poor stomach will cease churning out all that acid.

I ACCEPT NOTHING BUT PERFECT HARMONY IN MY MIND AND BODY. I RETAIN CONTROL OF MY LIFE BY SLOWING DOWN—SLIPPING INTO SLOW MOTION FOR A TIME.

THANK YOU, FATHER, FOR THE LESSENING OF TENSION, FOR THE QUIETING OF NERVES. I AM CALM, SERENE, AND TRANQUIL—LIKE A SKY-BLUE POOL IN THE EARLY DAWN.

BEGINNING WITH MY FACE AND TRAVELING DOWN MY BODY, I FEEL A RELAXATION OF MUSCLES AND THE RETURN OF CALM.

□ *INSOMNIA* □

The poor insomniac cannot fall asleep or cannot stay asleep, and sometimes suffers both symptoms. Insomnia is a ball of half-dried rubber cement rolling down a hill of leaves. It grows larger and larger and rolls faster and faster until sleep is merely a figment of the imagination. Insomnia becomes the enemy, and when human beings fight insomnia, they give it energy and stride into battle against it like gladiators. Of course sleep is impossible in this situation.

Most insomnia is caused by anxiety. It can also be caused by things as simple as pillows, mattresses, overheating, overcooling, poor ventilation, undue light or noise, too much coffee, too much activity, being too tired or not tired enough, tomorrow's problems, yesterday's problems, and tonight's. If you consider the awake time of insomnia as the enemy, then it becomes one—you make it real. When insomnia strikes, the first thought human beings have is, Quick, get back to sleep! That may not be the answer. Trying to go back to sleep in a hurry is similar to putting socks on a chicken. Can't be done: once you focus all your energy into getting back to sleep, your muscles tense, your eyes squinch up, and your entire body becomes rigid.

The first key to good sleep is letting go. If you let go of the irritation you feel at not being able to sleep, you lessen insomnia's impact. Let go of the worry that you won't fall back to sleep. As a matter of fact, let go of all negative thoughts, feelings, worries, tension, and stress. Be easy in your mind.

Blue is the color of reflection and coming-to-terms. Blue energy is acceptance, not hostility. We know many people who immediately look at the clock when insomnia strikes; they count the hours till dawn or until the alarm goes off. They fret that they'll get only four hours of sleep, or three, or six. They worry that they'll be tired the next day or that their eyes will be red or puffy. They desperately try to fall gently back to sleep.

Concentrate on Blue's energy. Blue sheets and bedding help. A soft Blue light bulb in the bedside lamp offers help. Picture a softly rolling Blue sea whose waves gently rock, rock, rock-a-bye the cradle. Visualize a deep Blue twilight and birds nestling for the night. Let Blue's soothing energy ease your troubled mind.

I GIVE NO ENERGY TO WORRY OR STRESS. MY ANXIETY AND INSOMNIA MELT AWAY.

THANK YOU, FATHER, FOR THIS TIME OF CONTEM-

PLATION. IN THE QUIET OF THE NIGHT, I REFLECT AND CONSIDER. I LOVE THE NIGHT AND ITS COMFORTING ARMS.

SLEEP IS NATURE'S MEDICINE. IT COMES TO ME AND GENTLY SURROUNDS ME. MY EYES ARE HEAVY, MY BREATHING DEEP AND FREE.

□ *NERVES* □

Long ago, women would whisper about one another at quilting bees: "She's just got 'nerves,' you know " or "All that's the matter with him is a case of the 'nerves.' " A disorder of the nervous system can range from chronic anxiety to an out-of-control psychosis. Every one of us has experienced a case of the "nerves" at one point or another. The nerves are the pony express riders of the body, constantly carrying information to the brain about the state of the body and its relation to the world. The brain itself contains over twelve billion nerve cells, each of which are linked to a zillion others; we depend upon the brain to integrate and assimilate the information the nerves convey to it.

At any given point in the day, the brain registers a multitude of nerve reactions, including but not limited to apprehension, displeasure, delight, contempt, joy, humor. Sometimes we even experience "mixed emotions," a combination of nerve reactions to outside and inside stimuli. The nerves also send information about the body's physical state, but the common syndrome of "nerves" is mostly connected to the mind and emotions.

You can control the content of those messages. Your case of anxiety or "nerves" can be cured by simply controlling the content of your thoughts. Yellow is the color of mental faculties and it refreshes and renews the nervous system. When you become aware that the nerves are sending messages of depression, anxiety, or imbalance to the brain, channel your energy into taking control. Light a Yellow candle and allow its subtle etheric energy to awaken the intellectual capacity of the brain—affirm that the brain is in charge of this aspect of living and that the brain controls thought content. Visualize confidence, serenity, and comfort. Affirm good health throughout the body via the nerves; tell the nerves to send messages of calm strength and relaxation. Regain control.

I SEE COOL QUIET. I FEEL COMPOSED AND CALM. MY MIND ENVISIONS A SURCEASE OF CHURNING ENERGY AND SEEKS THE TRANQUILLITY OF LIFE.

THANK YOU, FATHER, FOR MY FUNCTIONING MIND . . . FOR THE POWER TO CONTROL MY THOUGHTS . . . FOR THE PEACE AND SERENITY OF MY EXISTENCE.

□ *SKIN CONDITIONS* □

It is natural that the beautiful, life-giving Yellow sun has much influence on the largest organ of the body: the skin. Except for the brain, the skin is the most complex organ. It continually renews itself by casting off dead cells and replacing them with new ones. The skin is efficient, and it will mostly take care of itself unless it is abused. It has built-in methods to take care of its own moisture and lubrication, heating and cooling the body, disposing of secretions and poisons through sweat, protecting the body and growing hair, cleansing its own pores, and holding the insides of the body together in a neat package.

The most important thing we can do for the skin is to leave it alone. Don't overexpose it to the sun, don't slather it with "beauty" preparations, don't cook it by scalding, don't freeze it in the snow . . . in other words, refrain from messing with it and, for the most part, it will take care of its own maintenance and production. The skin is an infallible indicator of inward dysfunctions. The skin exhibits spots when the body suffers from measles or the chicken pox; it turns blue when bruised; it manifests a rash (eczema) when the body and mind are stressed.

One well-known dermatologist tells his eczema patients, "When you get rid of the source of your stress, you'll get rid of the eczema." Once again we see that the mind profoundly influences the body. Lessen the stress and the body blooms with good health and all organs function smoothly. It follows that a body will live longer if stress on the mind and emotions is kept at a minimum. How can we control stress and thereby clear up skin problems? Begin with the mind.

Yellow is the color for all maladies related to the skin. Yellow affects nerve endings immediately beneath and resting on top of the skin. For some skin problems, expose yourself to a gentle ray or two of pure Yellow sunlight. Plant some buttery-Yellow daffodils and tend them. Rock gently in a Yellow hammock. Enjoy some Yellow roses or wildflowers. Paint your kitchen cabinets sunshine Yellow while affirming good mental and emotional health with your mind and voice—watch your skin glow!

MY LIFE IS BRIGHT AND GLOWING! I MOVE SMOOTHLY AND HAPPILY THROUGH THE DAYS, SPREADING "SUNSHINE" AS I GO.

THANK YOU, FATHER, FOR THIS MIRACULOUS BODY OF MINE, FOR THE COMPLEX AND WONDERFUL FUNCTIONS OF MY SKIN. MY SKIN BREATHES AND SHIMMERS. SILENTLY IT HEALS ITSELF AND WARNS MY MIND OF DANGER.

THE CREAMY, HEALTHY TEXTURE OF MY SKIN REVEALS ITSELF. OVER EVERY INCH OF MY BODY I EXHIBIT SHINING GOOD HEALTH.

□ *STOMACH ULCERS* □

Can't you just feel the acid churning in your stomach? Can't you feel the hot battery acid roiling around in your gut? Well, just think about what you've sent down the throat to be digested by this sensitive, complex organ! The stomach is routinely treated with disregard. We consume mountains of spicy foods; we immerse ourselves in emotional stress, precipitating or aggravating an already tender stomach. The result can be the dangerous stomach ulcer.

The definition of an ulcer will get your attention immediately: an eroded sore often discharging pus and other fluids; a place of infection or open wound. YUK! Gross! Gastric pain or distress is the most characteristic symptom, and the pain may vary between aching, burning, or cramping.

However, the bright side is that many ulcers will heal themselves if we give them half a chance. The primary treatment of stomach ulcers is the patient's responsibility. Easing of stress and tension, without the use of tranquilizers, is the most healthy goal people who suffer with stomach ulcers can achieve. The easygoing person seldom gives himself an ulcer.

We can do much to ease the pain of stomach ulcers. First, get a medical opinion and, if necessary, take the required medication. Follow recommended dietary changes. Parallel with this action, try to slow down and relax. Use the same protocol as persons with high blood pressure: seek balance and harmony. Green's healing energy can help with this. Green produces a calming effect on human beings by floating away stress and nervousness, and by reminding people of nature and its bounty.

Green rays are particularly helpful because, within a serene environment, the production of harmful stomach acids slows down. Surround yourself in a tranquil Green environment and feel the middle body ease.

I AM HARMONIOUS, POISED, AND SERENE. I LANGUISH IN NATURE'S GREEN HEALING BOWER. I AM ROCKED SOFTLY IN THE FATHER'S CRADLE.

THANK YOU, FATHER, FOR THE CONSTRUCTIVE USE OF MY BODY'S ENERGY. ALL MUSCLES RELAX, ALL PAIN IS BANISHED.

C H A P T E R X

PERSONAL LIFE AND BUSINESS LIFE

□ *CAREER AMBITION* □

Ambition is a dynamic power which fuels achievement. Blind ambition has become a catchphrase for those who are simply insensitive and uncaring. Real ambition provides satisfaction and fulfillment in your chosen work, for it is through ambition that we move upward from level to level. Career ambition enables us to gaze into the future, creatively visualize our success, and climb aboard the outbound triumphant express.

Ambition can be described in some cases as determination. Those who are determined to succeed rarely fail. Failure is permanent but defeat is only temporary. A former all-American football player was heard to state, "I never lost a game—sometimes I ran out of time, but I never lost a game." What a glorious way to view a career!

Healthy career ambition implies that the worker is always alert for learning experiences and new productive ideas. He is committed to excellence in his job performance. This vital career power begins in the mind. (Yawn. How many times have we written that phrase!) Career ambition moves steadily onward and upward by the setting and accomplishing of goals and by the stimulation of career motivation.

Yellow energy stimulates the mind and parents the desire and determination to succeed in the workplace. Yellow enhances creativity. These rays enlighten and illuminate. An office accented with bright Yellow is a fine place to toil. Yellow is a positive, optimistic color energy and can be utilized most effectively when applied to a job or career-related task. Concentrate on Yellow's energy and allow it to pick you up and power you down the road to complete success and happiness in your work.

I GLITTER AND SIZZLE WITH AMBITION AND PRIDE IN MY WORK. CREATIVE SOLUTIONS ARE IMMEDIATELY REVEALED! CONFIDENCE IN MY PROBLEM-SOLVING SKILLS AND MY MOTIVATIONAL EFFORTS PROVE POSITIVELY THAT I SUCCEED.

THANK YOU, FATHER, FOR THE POWER TO RAPIDLY ASSIMILATE INFORMATION AND PUT IT TO WORK ON THE JOB. MY MIND IS RAZOR-SHARP—NO GLOOMY OUTLOOK EVER!

EFFORTLESSLY, I MOVE STEADILY UPWARD IN MY CHOSEN CAREER. SUCCESS IS MINE!

□ *CREATIVITY AND IMAGINATION* □

Yellow color energy provides us with *such* a fertile ground for imagination and creativity. Yellow endows us with the ability to focus the mind, think clearly, and come up with a creative answer/invention/design. One way to make your dreams come true is to channel them through your imagination.

Stumped for an answer to a difficult question? Need a creative idea? In the market for a creative solution to a problem? Concentrate on Yellow's stimulating mental energy and wait for the answer to come. The Yellow candle flame will spur your imagination and entice your creative genius to activity.

The key to every worthwhile anything was once an imaginative thought in the mind of its inventor. A creative imagination is the one quality common to all great artists, business people, scientists, statesmen, musicians, and philosophers. The imaginations of the great thinkers and doers of all time created elaborate worlds in their minds. The human imagination knows no bounds; highly developed creative thinking mechanisms catapulted the great thinkers and doers into the spotlight. A healthy imagination grants an enthusiasm for life that will affect everything you do.

Through the purity of Yellow rays, you will find that you are creative too. Your imagination may have been stifled by negative energy for a time, but it's there in your mind, waiting to launch you into abundant, exciting life. The imagination is a never-ending river of creative thoughts and ideas. Set sail up that river and your life will spontaneously take a dramatic turn for the better. Guaranteed.

NEGATIVE ENERGY BEGONE! CREATIVE ENERGY COME HITHER! IMAGINATION SOAR!

THANK YOU, FATHER, FOR THE BEST AND BRIGHTEST MIND THAT THINKS CREATIVE, IMAGINATIVE THOUGHTS. I AM FLOODED WITH FANTASTIC SCENES, ANSWERS, INVENTIONS, SOLUTIONS!

OPEN UP THE GATES OF IMAGINATION—LET IN MY CREATIVE GENIUS! I'M READY TO FLY!

□ *DREAMS, DESIRES, AND WISHES* □

Dreaming and wishing are brainstorming in private. When we dream about, desire, and wish for things, we overcome natural tunnel vision and open up new vistas of possibilities. It is through our dreams that we find answers and give direction to our lives. What we desire and wish for on the most basic level of the subconscious, that is what the mind seeks to make possible in life.

To open up the pleasure palace of the mind, dream a little and wish for fantastic things. Make a picture of your dearest desire and seek to develop that picture in everyday life. Dreaming requires spiritual energy, and this energy has no limitations—all obstacles and limiting beliefs are gone and we can imagine whatever we please.

Rose emits this kind of spiritual energy. From Red we receive the blast of action energy necessary to move us forward to achieve our wishes, but from Rose we are allowed the privacy, the fantasy of visioning our dreams. Dreaming is necessary to keep the delicate balance of fantasy/reality alive in the mind.

Rose points the way to turn dreams into reality. It allows the mind to find ways to make wishes come true. Rose gives structure to wispy desires and vague yearnings.

Light a Rose candle and elevate yourself above the

mundane. Set your imagination free to dream and wish. Find ways to satisfy your desires.

MY MIND FLIES HIGH IN SEARCH OF MY DREAMS. I SEE VISIONS OF WISHES GRANTED, DESIRES MET.

I OPEN MY MIND TO ABUNDANT IMAGINATION—TO FANTASY. I REACH NEW HEIGHTS OF CREATIVITY. I EXPLORE, I TRAVEL THROUGH THE MISTS OF IMAGINATION AND FIND WAYS TO MAKE MY DREAMS COME TRUE.

THANK YOU, FATHER, FOR MY FERTILE, IMAGINATIVE MIND!

□ *HOPE* □

Merle Stein writes, "When there is no hope, there is no tomorrow, there is not even much to be said for today." She also tells us that when there is no hope, there is no fear. This means that if we choose not to hope, then we are willing to settle for what we have, the present, the status quo. Hope for something better tomorrow. Don't accept today's misery as the best life has to offer.

We believe that hope is as necessary to human beings as breathing is. We *must* hope, we must strive, we must stretch and reach and work. We simply cannot sink down into despair, into the quicksand of living death. Without hope, life is ashes and dust, and it is a crime to allow the precious gift of life to wither and blacken with indifference.

You cannot buy it and you cannot acquire it. You can't steal it and it cannot be given to you. You must have it and you must feel it. If you cannot conjure a little something to be hopeful about, then you must manufacture some little something. You must practice hoping. You must force yourself to see further than the end of your nose; you must reach for higher and better goals, more skills, more love, more compassion, more laughter, more goodness. Pretty soon you are in the habit of hoping and your feet will dance on the cobblestones of vibrant life.

Orange is the ray of hope and without it we cannot live. Orange is happy, healthy, positive, glowing with goodness and confidence. This energy lights up even the darkest corners of the mind, and widens the horizons. In the darkest hour, surround yourself with vital, pulsing, life-giving Orange color energy. Then take one baby step . . . may I? . . . yes, you may . . . and you must. Then take another, and another, and another . . .

THANK YOU, FATHER, FOR FAITH AND HOPE AND LOVE. YOUR ALL-SEEING, ALL-KNOWING LOVE HOLDS ME UP IN TIMES OF DESPAIR. I TAKE HOPE FROM YOU, FATHER, AND I AM A GRATEFUL RECIPIENT.

I DRINK DEEPLY OF THE TONIC OF HOPE—I SEE ITS GLISTENING, SHINING FRUIT WITHIN MY REACH.

I WILL HOPE. I WILL NOT GIVE UP. WHATEVER IT TAKES, I WILL ALWAYS HOPE.

□ *JUSTICE AND FAIRNESS* □

Justice is the practice of identifying persons for what they are and what they do and say, and treating them accordingly. It means to praise virtue, productivity, creativity, honor, and truth, and to withhold praise from cowardice, manipulation, criminality, and deceit. Being fair means rewarding those characteristics and traits that are pro-life, and condemning those characteristics and traits which are anti-life.

In making a fair judgment, man must remember that other men do not exist for his sake, as his servants or as his masters, and that we do not exist for their sake. Man must remember that "I want" does not mean "I am entitled to." Man is an end unto himself, and the just man—the "fair" man—will take only what he has earned and what he deserves, either materially or spiritually.

The principles of justice are always in action, whether we know it or not, and we are always making value judgments of others, our surroundings, situations, and circumstances. It is necessary for life that we cling to a code of morality which includes the highest standard of justice. Make your judgments free from improper influence or bias, and hold these words in the forefront of your mind: honesty, objectivity, impartiality, nondiscrimination, nonprejudicial.

Indigo energy helps man remain on point, to travel the straight and narrow, to judge each man by the same set of ideals. This spiritual energy promotes the essence of democracy and respect for the rights of other men. It enhances cooperation, decency, and fair play. Being near the end of the cool, electric, spiritual spectrum, Indigo works on intangible values and speaks to us in a spiritual way; it says live together benevolently, be civilized, be true to truth.

Judges sometimes wear deep Indigo robes instead of black. Intermediaries and arbitrators should too. Anywhere a value judgment is made, at any time or issue in life when a fair decision is required, Indigo energy should be present.

I HOLD TO THE VALUES OF FAIRNESS AND JUSTICE. I ORDER MY LIFE ACCORDING TO HONORABLE STANDARDS.

THANK YOU, FATHER, FOR THE FAITH TO DEPEND ON OTHER MEN AND THEIR JUSTICE AND FAIRNESS. THANK YOU FOR MAN'S OBJECTIVITY AND HIS CLEAR VISION.

I MAKE FAIR JUDGMENTS CONSISTENTLY, BY THE SAME STANDARDS, WITH THE SAME INCORRUPTIBLE VISION, FOR EVERYONE. I SEE ALL SIDES. I REMAIN TRUE TO TRUTH.

□ *OPTIMISM* □

There is never a good time to be pessimistic about anything, ever. You can be cautious and conscientious and thorough, but never pessimistic. Because, as we've said before, the mind will strive to develop the words-which-describe-the-picture-in-the-mind. Optimism is the inclination to put the most favorable construction on actions and events, or to anticipate the best possible outcome. Being optimistic does not mean being naive or silly. It simply *feels* better when you look for the good in every person and every situation.

Some people say they are optimistic, but really they are Pollyanna types: they chirp and giggle and simper—it's enough to make you gag. This is not optimism; it's ignorance and shallowness. The true optimist refuses to fail. He might face defeat now and again, but he refuses to give up and keeps looking for the "goody" life has to offer.

Consciously face your life according to the "best" standard; that is, prepare to do your part, produce the best product you can produce, expect the best, look for the best side of things, work for the best, believe the best, and determine to be the best person/mother/architect/dairy farmer/custodian/race-car driver you can be. The picture of "best" things will set itself in living color in your mind and your computerlike mind will do everything in its power to develop that picture in "real life."

Yellow, of course, is the color of the optimist with his sunshiny face and beaming smile. The mentally stimulating Yellow energy revs up the mind's power to aim high and move fast toward the best possible scenario.

Dye that old tablecloth—the one with gravy stains—a bright Yellow. Ditto with the ragged mow-the-lawn T-shirt. How about a Yellow throw pillow, even if it doesn't match your decor? Have a little fun with this cheerful color, and if you find yourself sinking into pessimism, quick get a Yellow candle and vanquish that dark mood.

THANK YOU, FATHER, FOR THE EXCITING, ENCHANTING FUTURE I FACE. MY LIFE IS CHOCK-FULL OF OPPORTUNITIES, WONDERFUL RELATIONSHIPS, HUGE SUCCESS, AND GREATNESS.

I BEAM WITH OPTIMISM—I CAN'T KEEP A SMILE OFF MY FACE! SEND IT ON, FATHER, I'M READY!

□ *ORGANIZATION, EFFICIENCY, AND TIME MANAGEMENT* □

Finding a place to start is the first step in getting organized. If your business and personal affairs are in a mess, the job of organizing them may seem overwhelming; you may want to gaze at the number of items to be organized with a sigh of defeat. Not to worry.

Tackle any organizing job by first making a list of small goals. ("Get organized" is not appropriate here.) For example, if your kitchen drawers are disasters, and you've dumped knives, forks, and spoons—plastic, picnic ware, everyday flatware, and silver—all in the same drawer, there are probably several jobs you want to accomplish at the same time. You might want to put all the plastic and picnic ware in the hamper or storage area; you might want to polish the silver before you put it away; you may want to incorporate the use of dividers in storing everyday flatware. So, make a list like this:

Take everything out of the drawer and make one pile;
Clean drawer;
Line with paper and put in dividers;

Separate pile into categories;
Box up picnic ware and store;
Lay silver to one side for polishing;
Put away flatware in sections;
Polish silver and store.

This is a tongue-in-cheek appraisal of the eating utensil situation, but notice the grain of truth.

Dwight simply cannot function without a list, or without several lists. Since he lives on a farm far from town, if he didn't make lists of things to do in town, he'd be making trips back and forth all day. And, when it comes time to take off in the RV, some necessary something might not get included; in the wilderness, a flashlight is something he doesn't want to leave behind. Dwight faithfully makes a list of small goals and evaluates his list every so often. Through the accomplishment of small goals, large goals are possible to reach.

The efficient use of time brings self-confidence. Wasting time leaves a bad taste; wasting energy does too. By seeking organization, your efficiency and time management will naturally improve.

If you are awash in a sea of disorganized junk, sit down by your Green candle, make a list with a Green pen, and simply begin with the first item and follow through. Green's energy provides a system of regularity to life; its watchword is balance.

IN THE QUIET, I MAKE MY MENTAL LIST. I SET SMALL GOALS AND ACCOMPLISH THEM ONE AT A TIME, CHIPPING AWAY AT ANY ENDEAVOR.

THANK YOU, FATHER, FOR THE COMPUTERLIKE METHODS MY MIND EMBRACES. I ORGANIZE, I DIRECT. CONFUSION BEGONE!

I AM ORGANIZED AND EFFICIENT; I MANAGE MY TIME

TO OPTIMUM EFFECT. I'M A MACHINE—A COMPUTER—A RUNNIN' LITTLE HONEY!

□ *OVERCOMING OBSTACLES* □

The more obstacles we overcome on the road to happiness and success, the more valuable the happiness and success. Having everything easy all the time makes us weak. Having to fight for the good of life gives us the tools to overcome any barrier, mental or emotional, physical or spiritual. It is a difficult truth, but struggle can be a creative force in life.

We can choose to look at obstacles as opportunities in disguise, and let's face it, if we didn't have "downs" we couldn't appreciate the "ups." Each victory over an obstacle makes us stronger and smarter when we meet the next. If we give up when we meet with resistance, then we have abandoned the fight for our happiness and success. There is no greater coward than one who gives up the battle for his own happiness.

Violet color energy is a spiritual plowhorse—it just won't quit pulling us upward and onward, over obstacles and obstructions. Violet rays help develop the stalwart traits that commend man to his fellows. Those who face obstacles boldly and bravely, and turn defeat into victory, are justly awarded honor by all. They are also the most useful and happy people around.

Violet says, "Got a problem? Hit an obstruction? Let's get by it!" This energy provides the maximum spiritual boost necessary to tackle an obstruction. Getting by a barrier just puts us one step closer to triumph. Don't fear obstacles—let 'em come! Take up the Violet flag of battle and meet those obstacles with courage. Violet has become a symbol of courage, so when you must deal with a problem at home or at work, be sure you have plenty of Violet energy around.

I DO NOT SHRINK FROM HARDSHIP, DIFFICULTIES, OR BARRIERS. I MEET THEM HEAD-ON. I WHIP THEM INTO SUBMISSION AND I GET BY THEM.

THANK YOU, FATHER, FOR THE LIGHT WHICH BEAMS THROUGH THE FIGHT. I MAY STRUGGLE, BUT I WILL TRIUMPH IN THE END.

I AM CAPABLE AND BRAVE. I MEET DIFFICULTY WITH POISE. I HANDLE OBSTRUCTIONS. I CRUISE BY BARRIERS. I LEAP OVER OBSTACLES.

□ *TRAVEL, SAFE JOURNEYS* □

Folklore of many cultures seems to home in on this bit of information: for safe travel and safe journeys, wear Blue. Sometimes we travel for pleasure and sometimes by necessity. In any case, if old wives' tales and folk medicine are believed, Blue energy must be present on a trip. Blue is a good energy for travel, however, because of its stress-free, calming assurance. Since Blue lessens anxiety, any journey would naturally be more enjoyable. Next vacation or next business trip, put on a Blue dress or a Blue suit and boogie.

MY TRIP IS SAFE AND ENJOYABLE. I DO NOT WORRY OVER NEEDLESS ANTICIPATIONS. I LOOK FORWARD EAGERLY TO MY JOURNEY.

THANK YOU, FATHER, FOR KEEPING ME SAFE ON MY TRAVELS, FOR WATCHING OVER ME AND PROTECTING ME. I FLY HIGH WITH THIS KNOWLEDGE.

C H A P T E R XI

WEALTH AND FORTUNE

□ *LUCK AND GOOD FORTUNE* □

Never discount the influence of chance or luck in life. Your good fortune may depend on accidental happenstance. But does it really?

Luck is considered a fluke, but many successful people say that they create their own luck. Good fortune also is considered the result of a positive accidental gamble. But an educated gamble is often a fortuitous opportunity to reap unexpected rewards.

You can attract good luck into your life. You must be alert and able to act on circumstances to your best advantage. Chance will always play a role in our lives—it is inevitable—and we must know when to take advantage of it. Be conscious of changing circumstances; watch for opportunities. If you venture nothing, you gain nothing. Risk provides advantage and the opportunity to win. If you risk incorrectly, you've given yourself a learning experience—just more information to file away. If you win, not only do you get information, but you receive positive good fortune.

Green is the color of luck and good fortune, and naturally so because when we think of good fortune we automatically think of finances. A lucky emblem—the four-leaf clover—is as Green as can be. Green reminds us of nature's abundant wealth. With this energy we combine the spiritual and the physical properties of life, culminating in a rewarding situation.

THANK YOU, FATHER, FOR I AM EVER ALERT FOR OPPORTUNITY! I MOVE PERFECTLY WITH THE COSMIC ENERGY OF THE UNIVERSE!

GOOD FORTUNE COMES TO ME! I AM A LUCKY DUCK! I TAKE ADVANTAGE OF THE MAIN CHANCE.

CHANCY SITUATIONS EVOLVE IN THE UNIVERSE EVERY DAY. I ACT ON FORTUITOUS OPPORTUNITY!

□ *PROSPERITY* □

Money: the frozen representation of our labor and trade, exchanged between men for the benefits and production of our minds. We never have enough of it or it slips through our fingers. We are frightened by debt, lack, and loss. Subconsciously, most human beings worry about money most of all. They fear it or worry about it because the money-is-the-root-of-all-evil warning, bastardized phrase that it is, has echoed through the halls of time. It is the love or lust for money, above everything else, that is evil. Not money itself.

Are you ready to hear something scary? The reason most of us worry about money is that we subconsciously believe that only a certain amount is appropriate to us, no matter how much we want or need. Sometimes we block ourselves and we hold the picture of a single-digit bank account in our minds. Consequently the mind seeks to fulfill this self-prophecy. Remove the obstacle and the picture of financial ruin and substitute a mental visualization of abundance. See yourself managing your money like a wizard, socking it away like a bandit. Imagine yourself awash in coin and currency. See yourself receiving checks and cash and dispensing them with intelligent, shrewd sense.

Green, of course, is the money color. Green energy is a magnet which draws prosperity to us. It represents victory over life's success barriers and opens the channel for abundant wealth. Change the mind picture of yourself anguishing over your checkbook to one in which you hunt places to spend money. Green rays help us to distribute wealth wisely under Grace in perfect ways. The Thwart Monster not only hoards money and withholds its wise dispensation, he tries to prevent money from coming into the hands of deserving human beings. In order to acquire more money, you must deserve to acquire more money; make yourself deserving and expect to receive that lovely Green money in exchange for the work you perform via the product of your mind and body. Use it to create joy, dispose of lack, avoid poverty, and provide comfort in your life.

MY CREATIVE MIND OPENS THE DOOR TO FINANCIAL SUCCESS. I SEE ONLY MONETARY ABUNDANCE. IT FLOWS TO ME IN STEADY, EVER-INCREASING WAVES.

THANK YOU, FATHER, FOR THE ABILITY TO DO WHAT IS NEEDED IN ORDER TO ACHIEVE MY FINANCIAL SUCCESS. I WORK, I CREATE, I DESERVE MY WORLDLY WEALTH.

MY SUPPLY IS INEXHAUSTIBLE AND IMMEDIATE—IT COMES TO ME UNDER GRACE IN MIRACULOUS WAYS.

CHAPTER XII

WORK RELATIONSHIPS

□ *ACCEPTANCE AND RESPECT FROM COWORKERS* □

In the workplace, all anyone really wants is to be accepted for who and what he is. We want to matter, to count for something, to feel important and needed. If we realize that others feel and want this same thing, it is easier to be understanding and work together. If a worker performs his job to the best of his ability, he will earn the respect of his coworkers, and vice versa. With a certain amount of time and effort, a respectful, accepting work situation can be established. Then, all workers harvest good feelings and self-worth from their production. A healthy, supportive working environment begins with the individual worker who demonstrates acceptance and respect for his coworkers.

Rose is the color energy which promotes this acceptance and mutual respect between workers. Workers can use this color in many ways: a bud vase and a silk Rose, desk sets, a Rose-colored lunch sack, wall hangings or locker decorations. Rose color energy in the common lunchroom or breakroom helps the work environment.

THANK YOU, FATHER, FOR THE CHALLENGE OF MY WORK. AND THANK YOU FOR MY COMPATIBLE COWORKERS. I ACCEPT MY COWORKERS IN THEIR MYRIAD AND MANY-FACETED VARIETY. I TAKE PLEASURE IN THE RESPECT I GIVE AND RECEIVE.

I WORK IN A FERTILE ENVIRONMENT, ONE WHICH STIMULATES ME AND EXCITES ME. I SEE MY FELLOW WORKERS STIMULATED AND EXCITED.

I RESPOND WITH RESPECT AND ACCEPTANCE TO MY COWORKERS. I RUSH TO ACKNOWLEDGE GOOD DEEDS AND GOOD WORK. I APPLAUD GOOD WORK.

□ *ADAPTING TO CHANGE* □

You might as well accept it: changes occur. Life is change. Change is learning. Change is necessary. For those who wish to remain cemented to one place/one level of knowledge/one set of problems and opportunities, read no further. For those who want to move upward, learn more, create more, do more, be happy, know joy and peace, you'd better learn how to adapt to change.

When you see a change a-comin' or you want to initiate a change, focus immediately on your own strengths. Mentally run through the list of experiences, skills, traits, and attributes that are well developed and reliable in yourself. Do not think about your weaknesses or anything pessimistic. After you have bolstered your self-esteem by concentrating on your strengths, adapting to change is not so scary.

Change opens doors. Change can reveal unknown riches, in yourself, in others, and in the world. Change can provide emotional independence. If you cling to one level of maturity in life, afraid to try or learn something new, you will always be dependent upon that level. Adapting to change requires you to use your strengths to choose, to act, to learn, and to accommodate a new set of facts, skills, and opportunities into your life path. Change does not require an abrupt about-face; it can mean only modification, alteration, transformation, variation, or slight adjustment. Don't be afraid of change. It's exciting!

Yellow is the color for adaptation to change. Yellow is not afraid of something new and different—its optimistic, creative energy pushes us to seek change rather than to hide from it. Yellow, with its happy, imaginative energy, removes negativity and fear. Those people who naturally wear a lot of Yellow and are drawn to Yellow clothing and decor, seem to exhibit a heightened awareness of change. They appear courageous and fearless. Wouldn't you like to be one of those people?

I DO NOT FEAR CHANGE—CHANGE IS POSITIVE AND EXCITING. I ADAPT TO CHANGING TIMES AND EVENTS SMOOTHLY AND CONFIDENTLY.

THANK YOU, FATHER, FOR LIFE'S OPPORTUNITIES TO CHANGE FOR THE BETTER. MY LIFE, MY RELATIONSHIPS, MY EXPERIENCES CHANGE MINUTE BY MINUTE—WITH LOVE, LAUGHTER, INFORMATION, WISDOM, AND SUCCESS FLOWING TOWARD ME LIKE A RIVER!

□ *COMMUNICATION* □

Have you heard the term "active listening" lately? Active listening is possibly the most important skill you can acquire in the workplace. It means that you actually hear what another says to you, not just with your ears, but with your mind. Sometimes this is hard work. We seem to think that we are really listening when we allow somebody else to talk. But that is not the case. Active listening engages the mind, ears, body, and consciousness.

To become a fully functional human being, we must listen and communicate with others who live on the earth. Through communication, we are alerted to danger and comforted in sorrow. Our most basic human needs are met through communication. Communication allows us to make friends and share knowledge.

Gold, the wise teacher, admonishes us to communicate with others, both at work and at home. Its energy prompts us to really listen to what our coinhabitants and coworkers are communicating to us. And Gold reminds us that we should always let others know what we need, and that if we do not, we cannot expect our needs to be filled. It's tit for tat, or the Golden rule.

NO DOUBLE-TALK FOR ME! NO VAGUE DEMANDS, NO LOPSIDED COMMUNICATIONS IN MY LIFE!

I COMMUNICATE BRILLIANTLY, GENTLY ALLOWING MY NEEDS AND DESIRES TO BE KNOWN. I COMMUNICATE BRILLIANTLY, RAPTLY LISTENING TO MY FELLOWS AND HEARING WHAT THEY WISH TO COMMUNICATE.

THANK YOU, FATHER, FOR MY COMMUNICATION SKILLS. THROUGH COMMUNICATION, I SEE THAT I AM CONNECTED—TO YOU AND TO MY FELLOW HUMAN BEINGS AND TO THIS BEAUTIFUL LIFE!

□ *CONSIDERATION OF OTHERS IN THE WORKPLACE* □

Apply the Golden rule. Treat others as you would like to be treated. We are each responsible for creating an environment of nonthreatening consideration in which to work. If you are observant, attentive, concerned, and courteous to those you work with, they will more than likely afford you the same consideration.

You catch more flies with honey, you know. Consideration of others brings people close and allows them the vulnerability to express new ideas. More is accomplished in an atmosphere of cooperation than an atmosphere in which conflict reigns and everyone works at cross-purposes.

Gold energy speaks to people in the workplace on a spiritual level: it fosters dignity and integrity, and it bolsters natural warmth and consideration among workers.

Human beings are frail and easily hurt, and thoughtless acts and deeds and the ignoring of another's pain or vulnerability make for a miserable existence, both for ourselves and our coworkers. The color Gold shows genuine concern for another, and it is demonstrated by an active show of appreciation and regard. In the light of Gold, remember to say "thank you" and "please."

Go to a garage sale or flea market and find a beautiful Gold-colored plate or tray. Set several Gold candles on it, and surround the candles with Golden leaves or dried flowers. Light your beautiful candles and invite several of your coworkers to share a cup of coffee and discuss work relationships. Watch the cooperation and consideration bloom!

I AM MINDFUL OF MY COWORKERS. I EXHIBIT POLITE BEHAVIOR. I KNOW WHAT IS THOUGHTFUL AND WHAT IS CONSIDERATE. I DEMONSTRATE MY REGARD.

THANK YOU, FATHER, BECAUSE I WORK WITH GRACIOUS PEOPLE AND WE ARE GENUINELY CONCERNED WITH THE WELFARE OF ONE ANOTHER.

I DEMONSTRATE CONTINUED AWARENESS AND APPRECIATION FOR THOSE WITH WHOM I WORK.

□ *COOPERATIVE UNITY AT WORK* □

Are you a team player? Do you look for a coworker's special abilities? Do you encourage the development of those abilities and add your specialties to the pot? Can you work in tandem with others toward a common goal? If you can, *presto*! Happy Working Conditions.

Or. Do you grumble when you don't receive enough credit? Do you snipe at coworkers or gossip behind their backs? Do you subtly sabotage another's contributions, make light of them, or scorn them? Do you disdainfully look down on your coworkers, knowing that you are more qualified? Do you think working toward a common goal is beneath you? Hmmmmmmmm. If you think any of these thoughts, does it surprise you that you are unhappy at your job?

Some tasks are simply too complicated to be accomplished by one person. Sometimes more knowledge and more hands are needed to put it all together. A team working together, skills meshing with skills, well-oiled parts working with other parts efficiently and easily, is optimum for productivity. Orange energy brings people together in cooperative unity. It helps a worker share with other workers, not in arrogance, but happily, productively.

The Orange rays help you develop good working relations with others, and since it is a social color, the fear of meeting and mixing with people is lessened considerably or eliminated completely. In areas where cooperative unity is prized or desired, use Orange energy to encourage it.

THANK YOU, FATHER, FOR OUR COLLABORATIVE EFFORT! THANKS FOR THE HARMONY AND RAPPORT OF OUR WORK.

I THROW IN WITH MY COWORKERS—I LEAD SOME-

TIMES AND FOLLOW AT OTHERS. I CONTRIBUTE TO THE SMOOTH FUNCTIONING OF OUR TEAM.

I AM INTERESTED AND CONCERNED FOR MY COWORKERS, AND THEY RETURN THE FAVOR. THANK YOU, FATHER, FOR THIS PRODUCTIVE UNION OF MINDS!

□ *GUIDANCE AND LEADERSHIP AT WORK* □

If your career is one in which you must train others and help them to develop, or if you are a trainee eager to learn a new job, leadership abilities are important. As in military training, the officer must first learn to follow before he can effectively lead others. The revered leader is one who guides his troops with love and kindness, always looking to further their lot and not to belittle or ignore their feelings. You can teach yourself to manage, supervise, and train others, to take them beyond their present potential. The follower who listens and acts on his supervisor's instructions, who thinks and figures, is a valuable asset to any job.

To enhance your coworkers' self-esteem and motivation, compliment them and reinforce their good qualities. Don't try to overcontrol or snap out orders like a Nazi. Pay attention when you give or receive instructions, think about those directions, and recognize the concept—the reason—behind them. We can all learn from one another; the strong leader learns from his charges.

Rose enhances leadership abilities. This fine energy promotes thoughtful responsibility and a caring attitude toward those under command. Rose wants to serve and serve well, whether it be an idea, person, or the self-image. Rose urges good daily work habits on leaders and followers.

Surround the command center in Rose and watch that job get done!

I LEAD WITH MERCY AND KINDNESS. I AM AWARE OF THE INDIVIDUAL PERSONALITIES OF MY TEAM.

I REINFORCE GOOD WORK HABITS. I RECOGNIZE TALENT. I FOSTER SELF-ESTEEM IN MY TEAM MEMBERS.

I LISTEN, FATHER, AND I HEAR AND ACT ON THE INSTRUCTIONS OF MY LEADER. I DISCOUNT PETTINESS AND KEEP THE FINAL GOAL IN MIND. I TAKE IDEAS ON LEADERSHIP FROM A GOOD LEADER; I RISE ABOVE POOR LEADERSHIP.

THANK YOU, FATHER, FOR THIS INVALUABLE OPPORTUNITY TO LEARN AND GUIDE.

□ *LOYALTY* □

Loyalty, like respect, is an honor that has to be earned. It entails the recognition and confidence in your coworkers and implies that there is honesty and integrity in your dealings together. If you were alone on a deserted island, you wouldn't have the opportunity to be loyal to coworkers, but you, by necessity, must be loyal to life and hope. However, loyalty in the workplace involves a network of people who rely on each other. Some coworkers need you to perform your job so that they can perform theirs, and the reverse is also true.

You must demonstrate loyalty: you must behave in such a way that others perceive you as someone they can count on, someone who is eager to get the job done, someone who puts the common goal ahead of petty grievances.

Rose is the ideal color energy for loyalty. Since being loyal is faithfulness to something to which one is bound by a pledge of duty, Rose strengthens the commitment and endows the worker with power to stand fast. Rose, with its spirituality, fosters allegiance and trustworthiness. Light a

Rose candle and resolve to earn the loyalty of your fellows and to give loyalty to those who earn it from you.

THANK YOU, FATHER, FOR THE STRENGTH TO STAND FAST, TO REMAIN TRUE, TO DEMONSTRATE MY LOYALTY.

I BEHAVE LOYALLY AND OTHERS REWARD ME WITH THEIR TRUST. MY COWORKERS SEE MY STEADFAST ALLEGIANCE AND THEY BEHAVE THE SAME.

THANK YOU, FATHER, FOR WE WORK TOGETHER, HANG TOUGH TOGETHER, AND EMERGE VICTORIOUS TOGETHER.

□ *SENSITIVITY IN THE WORKPLACE* □

Being sensitive to the people you work with is a rare attribute today. Most of us, without thought, trample upon the tender leaves of another's feelings and crush the new blossoms of their nature. It takes so little effort to be sensitive and aware; we can work against being callous and rejecting to the people with whom we labor. Being insensitive is a problem in the "relating to others" arena, and those insensitive oafs who are mean and stupid to their coworkers gain no respect and no acceptance—they are avoided like the plague. Coworkers erect fine defenses against them and choose to stay away, just to avoid having their feelings hurt through an unthinking boorish remark or action.

Be aware of the feelings of others; respond to their feelings gently. Light a beautiful Rose candle and offer your acceptance and acknowledgment.

Rose is a fine energy, one which intensifies sensitivity and heightens awareness in oneself and in others. One of

Rose's aspects is a desire to serve with deep compassion. Burn your Rose candle to foster sensitivity.

I AM FINELY TUNED TO THE FEELINGS OF MY FELLOWS. I NOTICE. I LOOK. I LISTEN.

I DISREGARD THE INSENSITIVITY IN OTHERS, FOR THEY ARE MORE TO BE PITIED THAN TAKEN SERIOUSLY.

THANK YOU, FATHER, FOR THE ABILITY TO BEAUTIFY MY WORLD WITH GENTLE, COMPASSIONATE CARING.

□ *SHARING KNOWLEDGE IN THE WORKPLACE* □

While it is impossible for one to share his ability with another, sharing his knowledge is easy. In the workplace, the common goal should always be considered when making plans and giving instructions. We must be big people, as leaders and as support staff; we must recognize that others have good ideas and talents that may not be readily apparent. We can learn so very much from our coworkers, for they have various backgrounds, experiences, training, and ideals. The think-tank idea was begun with this sharing of knowledge idea, and it has paid off handsomely for those people who are "big" enough to know they can learn from others.

Rose energy's purpose is to help others through kindness and caring. Rose seems to understand human emotions and appreciates them. Rose enhances beautiful and productive work relationships: if workers do not worry that they will be rejected or ridiculed or discounted, they are more eager to brainstorm and share knowledge. Rose promotes an atmosphere of calm and fertile sharing. It is neither threatening nor wicked.

To set up a situation in which workers share with workers, light a Rose candle to start the energy moving.

I REJOICE THAT I CONTRIBUTE TO MY JOB AND MY COWORKERS. I OFFER MY IDEAS AND MY PLANS. I LISTEN AS OTHERS OFFER THEIRS. I WORK WELL WITH MY FELLOWS.

THANK YOU, FATHER, FOR THE VARIED AND WONDROUS PEOPLE I WORK WITH! I LEARN SO MUCH FROM THEM! IN RETURN, I GIVE OF MYSELF TO THEM!

THANK YOU, FATHER, FOR THIS ABILITY TO SHARE KNOWLEDGE AND TO GROW!

CHAPTER XIII

FAMILY RELATIONSHIPS

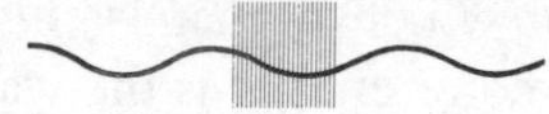

□ *AFFECTION AND LOVE* □

Affection comes from a Greek term, *agape*, meaning unselfish, active concern for the well-being of another. In the family, this affection is intended to be expressed as often as possible. Of course, since families are so intimate, there are times of conflict, crises, distress, and downright aggravation. But the family affection and love are always near the surface—they are resilient and fathomless. Family love is powerful, durable, and tough. Within the family, we are allowed to grow and change and are supported in our efforts to learn. Red is the color energy which encourages this exchange of love and support.

Relationships, careers, and finances may swirl like chocolate in a marble cake, but family affiliation is always present. To ensure this abundance of family affection, decorate with vibrant, sparkling Red, either with bright splashes of color in wall hangings or throw pillows or flower arrangements.

It has been said that a family is a "place that when you go there, they have to take you in." What a comfort to know that if life bloodies our noses and drives us to our knees, we can always find solace in the heart of our families.

This is a two-way street, however, and each family member must place the family's welfare near the top of the list of priorities. If you would be loved, love others. If you need support and affirmation, give them. If you need a shoulder to cry on, offer yours. To create and/or bolster family affection and love, understand that the family is a place where you and other members can be totally accepted, understood, respected, and trusted. The family is a nurturing environment which demands the exchange of love and affection. Red color energy is the wavelength of loving exchanges.

A beautiful way to use Red in this respect is a rose garden. Deep, rich Red roses can be cultivated in a flower pot or a big backyard. Artificial flowers in Red brighten any room or family area. Red symbolizes a strong love, a strong emotion, and power for the demonstration of affection and regard. This color energy is gay and stimulating and reminds us of the wonderful, supportive force of family love.

THANK YOU, FATHER, FOR MY FAMILY. FOR THE LOVE AND AFFECTION WE SHARE. FOR THE NURTURING, ACCEPTANCE, AND TRUST WHICH FOUNDS OUR FAMILY ON A COMMON GOOD.

I LOVE MY FAMILY AND I EXPRESS THAT STRENGTH IN AFFECTIONATE, AFFIRMING ACTS, WORDS, AND DEEDS.

MY FAMILY RELATIONSHIP IS INVIOLATE. I WORK TO KEEP IT STRONG AND HEALTHY. I AM REVITALIZED BY GIVING AND RECEIVING LOVING COMMUNICATION.

□ *BLESSINGS IN THE HOME* □

It pleases the Father when His children live in harmonious, peaceful environments. A loving family is truly a blessing.

Anything we thank and praise the Father for is a blessing. There can be no more security in the world than a nurturing, positive family environment.

Blessings are events which change the course of life in positive ways. Even some events which we believe are negative can be opportunities to reap blessings. A thankful spirit produces blessings effortlessly, and White is the energy that attracts blessings to life. One who insists on counting his blessings, and thinks about the good things of life always, has invited additional blessings to himself. White's ray is the path along which great blessings reach us.

White makes it possible for us to understand that blessings always outnumber problems; it gives human beings the wisdom to know this. A positive, self-perpetuating practice is to stop and look around at the home and family every day. Make it a habit to give thanks for blessings. Spend no energy on cursing the bad times of life. Positive energy attracts more positive energy.

MY HOME IS BLESSED. HAPPINESS AND SUCCESS COVER MY HOME LIKE A WARM, SAFE BLANKET.

THANK YOU, FATHER, FOR MY BLESSINGS . . . FOR EVER-REPLENISHING VITALITY AND HAPPINESS.

I LOVE MY LIFE AND MY HOME—I ATTRACT EVER-INCREASING BLESSINGS TO MY HOME AND FAMILY.

□ *COMFORT* □

When you are having a hard time and the Thwart Monster takes his good ole time getting away from you, a little comfort saves the day. When you've made a mistake and you quiver on the edge of the Without Syndrome swamp, a little comfort comes to the rescue. Comfort soothes your frazzled nerves and lets you know that you are okay, that you've hit a snag, and that you'll be back on your feet in no time a-tall!

At these times, we all need a little comfort and a little space. We need the relief from battle in order to refresh ourselves. We need to be comforted just as we need to comfort others. Gold's function is to radiate comfort to all who come in contact with its radiant light.

Have you ever stood and contemplated a picture of religious significance? It is the great painter or artist who can communicate the subject's ability to comfort and protect. It takes little talent for man to acquire the skill of comforting others; comfort is simply the dispensing of compassion and soothing ministrations to another about whom we care.

Next time you run into heavy weather and you need a little comforting, wrap yourself in a warm Gold blanket or afghan. This closeness and warmth will perk you up right away. Learn to needlepoint, like Roosevelt Greer, the great football player. Ask your great aunt Hattie to make you an afghan! Chances are she'll be delighted. Buy her the yarn and make sure to purchase several Golden skeins!

I DO NOT INDULGE IN SELF-RECRIMINATION; I DO NOT DWELL ON MY MISFORTUNE. I ACKNOWLEDGE IT AND I MOVE ON.

THANK YOU, FATHER, FOR THE ABILITY TO ACKNOWLEDGE MY LESS-THAN-DELIGHTFUL STATE OF BEING . . . AND FOR THE ABILITY TO KNOW THAT IT IS ONLY TEMPORARY.

I COMFORT MYSELF AND I OFFER COMFORT TO OTHERS. COMFORT IS A RESPITE, AN OPPORTUNITY TO REGROUP AND REST.

□ *FAMILY HARMONY* □

Remember the Capulets and the Montagues? Romeo and Juliet were doomed because of dissension in the family ranks. Not only did these two Shakespearean families feud like the Hatfields and the McCoys, they even fought among themselves. As the English say, "My, what a sticky wicket!"

Family harmony can be achieved easily, as long as family members realize that there will be disagreements, arguments, and spats. These workings at cross-purposes are only temporary, though, in a family that prizes harmony, because all the members know that the love between them is not threatened and that care and concern for one another lie just beneath the surface. A family is a network of people supporting and validating the other members; one member does not have to submerge his "self" to help create a harmonious, loving environment. He can still retain his individuality. He can even bloom and grow in his own direction, all the while receiving love, support, and comfort from his family.

Family harmony is giving and receiving, supporting and asking for support, sharing and teaching, learning and reaching. The family should be a loving, organized system, flooding one another with confidence, encouragement, and love. Orange is naturally at the center of this happy crowd. This energy explodes and zips from one to another, laughing here and boosting spirits there.

In the family room, decorate with splashes of Orange and revel in the good feelings emitted from its rays.

REGARDLESS OF OUR DIFFERENCES, I EMBRACE MY FAMILY UNIT. WE WORK HARMONIOUSLY TOGETHER LIKE A BEAUTIFUL SYMPHONY OF LOVE.

I CONTRIBUTE TO THE HEALING PEACE OF MY FAMILY, AND THEY SHELTER ME AND PROTECT ME.

THANK YOU, FATHER, FOR THIS MUSICAL COMBINATION OF TONES AND CHORDS WHICH MAKE UP THE MUSIC OF MY FAMILY LIFE.

□ *FAMILY UNITY AND ENVIRONMENT* □

The traditional family is all but extinct in our society. Times have changed, for the better or worse we cannot say at this point, but now it appears that all family members travel in different directions. It is hard to maintain a strong, unified family environment. Each family now is unique and requires unique measures in order to create a stable environment. It can be done, however, by becoming alert to each member's major needs.

One major need of family members is warmth. With a dozen items to take care of, with time schedules planned to the final second, taking time to share warmth of feeling, to express love and concern, is short. It is necessary to take this precious time, though, and even the habit of ending every conversation with "I love you" helps bridge the gap and draw family members together.

Families also need to feel that each is an integral part of a whole. It is a basic human need to feel that we are a part of something valuable, and to feel that our presence is desired. The family is "we," not "I."

The easiest way to enhance this warm, safe, affirmative environment is to speak the words. Tell the other, in words, how important they are, how much we love them, how we feel concern for their welfare. Indigo represents the sharing of a warm intimacy with sensitive and loving family members. Indigo energy promotes a healthy family environment.

Indigo removes the embarrassment some people feel when they speak loving words. Words of praise and love are balm to the wound. How wonderful it is to hear "I'm proud of you," "I can depend on you," or "I think you're great."

To create a unified, supportive family environment, speak frankly to one another, say the words of love, and protect the haven. Work toward enhancing an environment where family members can come for comfort, development, and regeneration. Indigo energy is charged with the power to banish outside pressures, forces of division, indifference, and emotional constipation. In the family room or wherever family members gather, use Indigo to aid in unifying the group and easing tensions. A strong family unity is a valuable investment for the future.

MY FAMILY IS POSITIVE AND FILLED WITH LOVING LIGHT. WE WORK TOGETHER, WE RESPECT ONE ANOTHER, WE LOVE EACH OTHER.

THANK YOU, FATHER, FOR THE SAFE HARBOR OF MY FAMILY. MATERIAL GOODS DO NOT MATTER, FOR IN THE ARMS OF MY FAMILY, I AM RICH BEYOND MY FANTASIES.

WE STAND TOGETHER. WE PROTECT THE LOVE WE FEEL FOR ONE ANOTHER. I WORK TO KEEP MY FAMILY CLOSE.

□ *HAPPINESS AND CHEERFULNESS* □

Happiness is an attitude or a state of mind. It is not the accumulation of material wealth or the lessening of tension or the absence of pain. It is an attitude you can cultivate regardless of your possessions or outer circumstances. Happiness is a state of pleasure, satisfaction, content, and delight. It is the Golden light of joy.

Man is a moody creature and some of us seem to deliberately embrace misery. You can cultivate a cheerful disposition and pass it along to your sullen brothers and sisters. Cheerfulness is contagious! A cheery countenance and attitude chase away pessimism and depression.

You can choose to be happy. Yes, you can. You can operate your life functions so you experience inner peace, tranquillity, and serenity. We must each define happiness for ourselves and experience it according to our own uniqueness. The first step in becoming a happy person is to speak the words, "I am happy!" If you say it and feel it, your mind seeks to develop that happy picture.

The natural physical expression of happiness is laughter. Laughter depicts a life lived abundantly and happily. We do not refer to maniacal mindless cackling; we suggest an explosive demonstration of merriment. Solomon tells us that "A merry heart doeth good like a medicine." Look for the fun in any endeavor; look for wit, cleverness, gaiety, and mirth! Seek laughter and joy.

Gold is the energy which emanates from happy people. It is the color of pleasure and delight. Isn't life a beautiful gift? And are we not responsible for living it happily and healthily? And doesn't laughter make us grateful to be alive?

Gold rays provide the energy to laugh and to enjoy ourselves.

I AM A HAPPY PERSON, FATHER! I LAUGH, I LOVE, I GIGGLE, I GUFFAW! I SEEK HAPPY PEOPLE, HAPPY SITUATIONS, AND HAPPY GOLDEN SUNSHINE!

I DEMONSTRATE MY HAPPY STATE OF BEING CONSTANTLY! NO MISERY FOR ME! THANK YOU, FATHER! I CHOOSE TO BE HAPPY! I CHOOSE TO SPREAD GOOD CHEER WITH MY WORDS, MY ACTIONS, AND MY INNER HAPPINESS.

□ *MAKING PEACE, FORGIVING* □

Discord and disharmony in the family bring destruction upon the individuals therein. A little disagreement is good, for it opens the consciousness and provides a possible learning experience, but consistent war between family members promotes revenge and malice. These dark feelings personify the Thwart Monster at its most terrible.

Praise be for the peacemaker, the one who settles a fight, the one who pacifies and arbitrates. Indigo is the cape of the mediator and peacekeeper. An argument or fight is pulsing with raw, coarse energy, and sometimes the combatants forget the love lying beneath the conflict. The peacemaker uses Indigo energy to remind the warriors of the basis for relationships, the love each holds for the other even in disagreement.

In any relationship there are times when we need to forgive, just as we need to be forgiven. For little things, like insensitivity, boorishness, and thoughtlessness, a forgiving nature brings humanity and wisdom to life. To forgive and be forgiven for our transgressions utilize the same dynamics. It is a letting go, a release of negativity. The relief in being forgiven or forgiving is incredible.

Indigo color energy allows us to see the harsh statement, the unfeeling criticism, the thoughtless act as a temporary mistake, not a lasting situation. The one who never commits these mistakes has not been born, so we must cultivate the habit of forgiving little slights—not ignoring them or overlooking them—but making our feelings known and then forgiving. This is a spiritual act and Indigo reminds the parties that people are not perfect and that momentary discomfort is not destructive.

Indigo points out that an isolated act of thoughtlessness is an opportunity to find new depths in ourselves, more compassion, and new possibilities for relating in the future.

The one who commits the mistake finds that being too proud to ask forgiveness is a severe self-limiting behavior. Indigo focuses on the challenge of honest evaluation and confrontation. It seeks to make peace and understand. David Augsburger writes of Indigo's message: "Forgiveness is letting what was, be gone; what will be, come; what is now, be."

Indigo energy cleans up the aura and provides great warmth and spiritual healing power. It soothes, reunites, and re-creates.

I FORGIVE SMALL INDISCRETIONS—I'M A "BIG" PERSON, NOT PETTY. I AM QUICK TO LET BYGONES BE BYGONES.

THANK YOU, FATHER, FOR THE ABILITY TO EXCUSE, TO PARDON, TO FORGIVE. I MAKE PEACE, FATHER, FOR WITHOUT IT WE ARE LOST IN DISCORD.

I BLOT OUT REVENGE AND MALICE. I TURN MY BACK ON DISHARMONY WITH THOSE I LOVE. I MAKE PEACE. I FORGIVE.

□ *OPENNESS AND COMMUNICATION IN THE FAMILY* □

Good communication is necessary in order to maintain a safe and secure relationship within the family. A close family should act as a safety net: within it, you should know that you are cared for and welcome, and that if you feel frightened or vulnerable, you can communicate this to your family. They would not ridicule or deliberately hurt you—or they shouldn't.

Each family member must nurture the lines of communication within the family; these lines must always be open. Each member must give time and attention, loyalty and support to the family communication system. You might not be able to run in and blurt out your concerns at any time, but you'll know, eventually, that the opportunity to express your views, concerns, and problems will be heard.

Openness in the family consists of words, touching, laughter, and all the other forms of communication—a cocoon of caring. Gold energy stands fast to protect this cocoon and it encourages the family to act as one unit. Gold rays offer the openness of shared feelings and the sharing of life's experience. This color should be prominent during family counsels and in one-on-one discussions.

A beautiful flower arrangement of dried Golden wildflowers picked from the side of the road enhances a family room. Brass accents enhance any decor. Upholstery with a Gold thread is enough to remind the family of the necessity of open communication.

I SHARE MY FEELINGS WITH MY FAMILY—MY FAMILY DEPENDS ON ME TO COMMUNICATE HONESTLY AND OPENLY.

THANK YOU, FATHER, FOR THE LUXURY OF OPEN COMMUNICATION IN MY FAMILY. WE HUG, WE TOUCH, WE LAUGH TOGETHER.

I AM SAFE IN THE BOSOM OF MY FAMILY, AND WE COMMUNICATE WITH ONE ANOTHER GRATEFULLY AND SAFELY.

□ *PRIDE AND WARMTH* □

Pride of self is necessary for healthy self-esteem. To be proud of your accomplishments and the product of your mind grants permission for you to keep on truckin', to aim for greater accomplishments. Also, being proud of someone you care for grants the relationship greater depth and satisfaction. Pride in another's accomplishments only makes you deeper, smarter, kinder, and better.

Pride must be expressed warmly. To withhold praise of another's good achievement is a moral ingratitude. You expect praise when you accomplish a difficult task, don't you? And rightfully so. So don't begrudge another his justifiable pride in himself and don't withhold your warm acknowledgment of his achievement. Then you will be worthy of pride of self and the demonstration of warm acknowledgment from others.

Gold energy helps develop this sincere interest in others, and makes it possible for you to exhibit warmth and pride in them. This demonstration makes you a more effective, more loving individual. A good measure of how warm and gracious you are is demonstrated by how you give and receive compliments. Just say "thank you" and express your delight in the recognition. Be quick to voice your admiration for another's accomplishments.

Gold rays speak these profound feelings of warmth and pride, and its energy allows us the freedom to feel pride, in ourselves and in others. If you feel pride in yourself, you are more likely to strive for greater goals; if you express pride in another, he is more likely to attack and conquer greater goals. Awards of accomplishment are expressed by Gold medals—Gold is the premiere acknowledgment of achievement.

I AM PROUD OF MYSELF AND PROUD OF MY ACCOMPLISHMENTS. I HOLD MY HEAD HIGH AND MY FACE SHINES WITH GOLDEN LIGHT.

THANK YOU, FATHER, FOR MY TALENTS AND ABILITIES. THANK YOU FOR THE DRIVE AND INITIATIVE I POSSESS.

I ACKNOWLEDGE WITH PRIDE THE ACCOMPLISHMENTS OF OTHERS. I WARMLY EXPRESS MY REGARD. I PRAISE THEM FREELY AND DESERVEDLY.

□ *PROTECTION IN FAMILY RELATIONSHIPS* □

Occasionally, the armor of the family is threatened, either by internal strife or by external forces. It is during calamitous times that the family relationship must stand its strongest. An assault on family unity is a serious threat to the well-being of all family members, and it requires a powerful concentration of energy to withstand a negative occurrence.

In one family, a son was arrested for passing a hot check. He had made a serious mistake and he was sentenced accordingly. Throughout the arrest, trial, and aftermath the family stood firm. "We love our son," they said, "but we recognize his transgression. He will pay his price, and while he does, our family will love him and will wish him well." Occasionally family members make errors, within the family unit and in the outside world. But the family is a haven, a place of serenity when we stump our collective toes in the world. The family ought to be one place where we can "work without a net."

Sometimes the family fights on a bloody battlefield when it seems that every person in the family is unreasonable, irrational, belligerent, thoughtless, and wasteful. We will fight among ourselves, but when an outside force threatens the family unity, all rise as one to protect the unit. Red's defiant energy is a big plus for this problem. These energy rays inflame the spirit and call forth reserve strength.

The family is a cohesive group with strong, affirmative power in the life of each individual. It is important to endure the hard times of life within and without the family, and to protect it with any weapon we can call upon. When the family must present a unified front, somebody needs to wear Red and to carry a Red banner of family protection. To protect the family, use Red candles to decorate the table and serve the meal on a Red tablecloth or Red place mats. Call upon Red color energy and its strengthening rays.

THANK YOU, FATHER, FOR MY FAMILY. WE WORK OUT OUR PROBLEMS IN AN ATMOSPHERE OF LOVE AND HARMONY. I MAKE PEACE WITHIN MY FAMILY.

I LISTEN. I HEAR. I SPEAK THE TRUTH. I AM GENTLE AND CARING; I NURTURE AND CULTIVATE THE LOVE IN MY FAMILY. I PROTECT THEM.

NOTHING CAN HARM MY FAMILY, FOR OUR FOUNDATION IS MUTUAL LOVE AND RESPECT. IN THE LIGHT OF TRUTH AND UNDERSTANDING, MY FAMILY IS STRONG AND UNITED.

CHAPTER XIV

ROMANTIC LOVE

□ *ATTRACTION—MAGNETIC APPEAL* □

Some people possess charisma, which is an involuntary, natural attraction felt for someone for no apparent reason. But there is a reason: it is because the charismatic person believes (and demonstrates) that he deserves to be loved, that he is willing to love, and that he has qualities which are attractive to other people—he portrays himself as one who is warm and loving. The voodoo charm some people seem to exude is only this feeling of self-worth.

The allure of a captivating person speaks to us on a spiritual level. What draws us near is the healthy, positive self-image held by the charismatic person. You have charisma and magnetic appeal also. If you feel good about yourself and send out vibratory messages that you desire love and interaction with others, they will intrinsically hear this call and gravitate toward you.

Rose, of course, is the color of magnetic appeal between human beings. Rose says, "I'm approachable, I'm nonthreatening, I embrace love, caring, and reason." Rose lets others know that you desire to be loved, and with this message snugly inside their hip pockets, people view you as an inviting, gregarious sort, and they approach, expand, feel good, and take pleasure in your company.

If you expect people to love you, they will, and they'll be drawn to you by your magnetic appeal. Light your Rose candle and enjoy the crowd of convivial, loving people who gather round you.

I LIKE WHO I AM AND I SHOW IT, NOT WITH SWAGGERING ARROGANCE, BUT BY MY PLEASANT COUNTENANCE, MY WARMTH, AND MY IRRESISTIBLE PERSONALITY.

THANK YOU, FATHER, FOR MY MAGNETIC APPEAL—I CALL FOR LOVE TO APPROACH ME—I AM AVAILABLE AND READY TO LOVE, SHARE, AND GIVE.

TRUE LOVE IS ATTRACTED INTO MY LIFE. I RECOGNIZE IT. THANK YOU, FATHER!

□ *ENCOURAGEMENT* □

Sometimes all we need in order to complete a difficult task is a little encouragement—a little boost from somebody else who acknowledges our struggle and expresses faith in our ability. And sometimes all the warrior needs is a nod of recognition from us; it allows the warrior to fight his battle with renewed energy.

Encouraging someone else costs us nothing. The few words of encouragement can mean so much to one who is striving to accomplish a goal or get through a crisis. All it requires of us is the observation and acknowledgment that our fellow human beings deserve encouragement.

Haven't you been given new heart in a dire emergency by some onlooker who said, "You can do it!" In a contest, haven't you been encouraged simply by applause or some other demonstration of acknowledgment? The Gold medal of victory seemed so much more attainable if your struggle was noted and supported.

Gold rays speak volumes of encouragement. Try an experiment: the next time you see someone struggling or seeking to achieve some goal, just say, "You can do it" or "Go for it." Note the look on the struggler's face; see his unspoken thanks. Bestow the Gold award of merit and encouragement to one who strives to achieve. Grant yourself a few encouraging words of faith. Step up on the platform of victory and award yourself the Gold medal!

I LOOK FOR WAYS TO EXPRESS ENCOURAGEMENT AND FAITH IN OTHERS. I FIND WAYS TO SAY, "YOU CAN DO IT" AND "COME ON" AND "ALL RIGHT!"

THANK YOU, FATHER, FOR THE KNOWLEDGE THAT YOU ARE ALWAYS ENCOURAGING ME, THAT YOU ALWAYS HAVE MY BEST INTERESTS AT HEART.

□ *FIDELITY AND VIRTUE* □

Virtue is goodness, morality, rightness, and loyalty. The word implies the highest of ideals in thought, word, and deed. Fidelity is the quality of being faithful, of remaining true to truth. It is a constancy to a pledge or vow, an allegiance which transcends daily life and is held to a degree of devotion above the common mean.

True virtue is a joyful thing. True morality stirs in man the rapture of perfect life. Virtue is kept from no one; it is available to all, accepts all, invites all. Virtue selects neither fame nor fortune but looks at the beauty of the soul. Human beings are able to cultivate a virtuous life, and the greatest happiness and success of all go to the human being who practices his virtues consistently.

No pain is ever as sharp as that experienced by one

who has been betrayed. Fidelity is in short supply today; man appears to accept the tenet that events dictate faith and that changing circumstances impact fidelity. Not so. Fidelity is the path to trust, and trust is the single most perfect virtue we can give or receive.

Nowadays we consider fidelity in connection with the commitment of one partner to the other in a marriage or love relationship. These relationships are so vulnerable to man's fits and starts; reliability and dependability are much desired but little demonstrated. If human beings go against the virtue of fidelity, trust is completely broken, and the foundation of the relationship has been painfully and violently smashed. Man can inflict so much anguish and pain upon another by being unfaithful.

White is a soothing, gentle energy which urges man to remain faithful and to practice virtuous living. These rays attract goodness and mercy, compassion and strength of mind. White reminds man that his actions must match his duty and vows; his virtue must match the way he manages his energy.

Broken trust brings anger, betrayal, pain, and a thousand other destructive emotions to a relationship. White's energy repels these evils. White says stop and think, count blessings, think of the possible outcome of faithlessness.

I AM TRUE AND LOYAL. I PRACTICE VIRTUOUS LIVING. I DEMONSTRATE MY FAITH AND MY FIDELITY.

THANK YOU, FATHER, FOR THIS RADIANT STATE OF EXISTENCE. I AM FAITHFUL TO GOOD AND I TURN MY BACK ON WRONGDOING.

I GIVE AND RECEIVE TRUST. I PROTECT MY FIDELITY AND MY VIRTUE.

□ *FREEDOM AND OPEN-MINDEDNESS* □

In a romantic relationship, failure to give one another space results in suffocation and feelings of being trapped. If one partner is overbearing and narrow-minded, the strain on love is stupendous. People are not possessions and they cannot be owned. Just as green plants cannot grow in a stultifying environment, people who love cannot grow, and, eventually, love withers and dies.

Partners must remain separate; this characteristic of genuine love should be preserved. One partner cannot be above the other and dominate the other.

How wonderful it is to be loved by someone who is standin' up and talkin' back! How proud it is to be loved by someone who is whole, healthy, productive, and flexible! What a poor love it is when we hold the regard of a dependent, stifled, noncreative whipped pup. How sad to see one partner as the consistent straight man while the other partner hogs the spotlight. Genuine love is not one partner impressing his ideas, his goals, his choices on the other. It is the liberal, generous, tolerant, open-minded partner who is loved for all the right reasons. The act of nurturing a partner's growth is an intimate practice.

Indigo enhances freedom from rigidly fixed preconceptions or ideas. It promotes the development of a mind open to new arguments or circumstances. Love needs freedom in every sense, and this energy brings an appreciation of the differences in lovers.

You can hear Regina brag about her husband whenever the subject comes up. She is terrible with numbers, but he is a wizard at managing money. She handles public relations and presents herself to the public like a pro. Gerald, the husband, shouts this to the world. He is confident enough in their love and in his own wholeness that he does not begrudge Regina her victories. Gerald encourages her to try new methods, branch out and expand, and to seek great goals by herself. Regina provides the same open-minded behavior as she gazes proudly at Gerald. Authentic love is deep and abiding here, and has been for twenty years. This couple believes that giving each other freedom to grow has to be the main contributing factor of their relationship's longevity and strength.

Coincidentally, this couple has decorated their home in Indigo. They have each stamped the seal of their separate personalities on the living quarters, but the main theme is Indigo. The room in which they plan and dream is rich with color and texture. Indigo in the bedroom enhances intimacy and makes it easy to respect individuality.

Indigo, this spiritual color energy, helps the lover perceive the beloved as a separate spiritual entity, and it allows the lover to encourage and affirm the being of the beloved. Although goals can be a commonality and the partners' ideals can be similar, Indigo reminds the partnership that open-mindedness and freedom only make true love grow. A love that is free is pure, and it finds its own path and travels in its own way.

I AM GENEROUS AND FORBEARING. I AM PROGRESSIVE AND DEMOCRATIC WITH MY LOVER.

THANK YOU, FATHER, FOR MY FLEXIBILITY AND MY CONFIDENCE IN MY LOVE. I AM NOT BOUND BY AUTHORITARIANISM OR NARROW-MINDED, FEARFUL EVENTS IN THE LIFE OF MY LOVE.

I FLY HIGH AND I ALLOW MY PARTNER TO FLY—IN HIS OWN WAY, AT HIS OWN PACE. I GLORY IN HIS SPUNK!

THE POSITIVE FORCE OF OUR INTIMACY NOURISHES OUR INDEPENDENCE. I HAVE AUTONOMY AND I ALLOW MY LOVER HIS AUTONOMY. I AM NOT THREATENED BY HIS FREEDOM—I AM PROUD.

□ *HONESTY, TRUTHFULNESS, AND PURITY* □

Honesty is the ability to reveal the truth at any time or in any situation. Truthfulness is the ability to verbalize these truths at any moment. Purity is the motivation that makes honesty possible, and then truthfulness. These attributes allow partners to feel secure in the knowledge that theirs is a healthy, lasting relationship.

There is never any reason to deviate from the truth. You may say that sometimes it is kinder to withhold the truth because it will hurt another. You give "another" very little credit for being a functional human being. The truth does *not* hurt. It purifies.

While we may have been conditioned over the years not to expect the entire truth or to expect an altered truth or just part of the truth, human beings should demand to be dealt with honestly. This process begins with ourselves. If we can deal honestly with others, this makes it okay for others to do the same with us.

White color energy recognizes this human need to trust and be trusted. White rays illuminate the honorable course and create a safe environment of unity and growth.

We can only become closer to the Father by clinging to veracity and by refusing to distort, avoid, or misrepresent the truth. The truth, revealed in the White light of pure spirit, must be our goal, no matter where it leads.

I AM HONEST AND TRUTHFUL IN ALL MY DEALINGS—I DON'T HAVE TO LIE. THE TRUTH IS ALWAYS CORRECT.

THANK YOU, FATHER, FOR THE GRACE OF THE TRUTH, FOR THE LIGHT OF THE SPIRIT, AND FOR THE STRENGTH OF REALITY. REALITY WILL NOT BE CHEATED.

I AM PRECISE, CANDID, AND ACCURATE. IT IS EASY FOR ME TO LIVE MY LIFE WITH HONOR.

□ *HONOR AND RESPECT* □

There is no reference book available that can teach you how to honor someone you respect, just as there is no handbook or manual available to teach you to behave honorably. Honor is the shining star of existence, and to feel it for someone else or for another to feel that you are honorable is the epitome of respect. Respect has been explained as the recognition for the separateness and the reality of another person. Honor is the award given to those who earn respect.

In any relationship, respect is the concrete slab of the success mansion. Remember the comedian who wails about never getting respect? And the songs that speak of wanting just a little respect? Partners must necessarily behave honorably in their dealings with one another, and partners must respect at least some aspect of the other in order to succeed.

Sometimes in a marriage, romance and infatuation fade, hopefully to be replaced by respect and honor. These things last and symbolize something that has been tested and proven, something that is solid.

If honor is the highest spiritual award we both bestow and receive, then Rose is the energy by which it is powered. Rose is that spiritual force that tells us what is honorable, what is valuable, and how we should behave. It focuses on high standards and high ideals. It showcases the best in us and in others, allowing us to respect ourselves and others. Rose energy lights up events and characteristics which deserve respect and honor.

If you feel a little off-balance and are having trouble

deciding what is the honorable thing to do, light a Rose candle and concentrate your mind. Go back to basics and do not compromise your code of morality.

I TAKE THE HONORABLE ROAD TO SUCCESS. I BEHAVE ALWAYS ACCORDING TO MY HONORABLE CODE OF MORALITY.

I KNOW RIGHT AND WRONG. I SEE WHAT IS CORRECT, WHAT IS ACCEPTABLE, WHAT IS REAL. I EARN THE RESPECT OF MY FELLOWS.

THANK YOU, FATHER, FOR THE OPPORTUNITY TO HONOR SOMEONE ELSE. I RECOGNIZE INTEGRITY IN ANOTHER AND I OFFER MY RESPECT.

□ *KINDNESS* □

Kindness is demonstrated by a special graciousness, a special warmth. It is not petty or insensitive. It is a feeling felt and expressed by one person for another which is based on love.

Remember how cruelly kids behave with one another, unintentionally? Our hearts cringe at the terrible things that are said and done during childhood. We refuse to view this as maliciousness, but immaturity displays little kindness. Concern and care for another is a learned skill. It is not lying down and being a doormat for some discourteous oaf. It is not subserving our right to happiness for the happiness of another, or putting off our goals in lieu of another's. Kindness is an attribute to be strived for highly, and it is high praise indeed to hear someone described as "kind."

Let us practice being kind to one another. So much pain, so many wounds, so much dysfunction in the world today could be helped by a little kindness. In the struggle to live, to love, to achieve, let us prepare an oasis of kind concern for our brothers. Maybe they will prepare one for us.

Gentle Rose guides us with its energy to kindness. A brutal man is not kind, but in Rosy light, a chord of tenderness can be struck. To receive kindness, you must be kind. Teach your children to be kind; teach your lover to be kind. Demonstrate kindness at every opportunity.

I SEARCH FOR GOOD IN EVERY PERSON, EVERY SITUATION. I AM KIND TO MY FELLOWS. I RECEIVE KINDNESS AND WARMTH FROM OTHERS BECAUSE I AM SO READY TO GIVE IT.

I PAUSE. I SEEK WAYS TO DEMONSTRATE MY KIND AND GENTLE NATURE. I REFRAIN FROM HARSHNESS.

THANK YOU, FATHER, FOR MY SWEET NATURE—FOR THE PLEASURE I RECEIVE FROM GIVING AND RECEIVING COURTESY AND KINDNESS.

□ *OVERCOMING TEMPTATIONS* □

Man, being what he is, will always be tempted to stray from the righteous path. He may be lured, decoyed, enticed, seduced, snared, or trapped. But all these "baits" are temptations and all promise difficult escape and a possible destruction of values. If man is committed to fidelity, he will say no to temptation.

It requires self-discipline to overcome temptation, and man is prone to succumb to a really tasty temptation, hoping that no one else will know. The fallacy in that thought process is that "no one else" cares if man succumbs, and the man himself and his Higher Consciousness are the only ones who will know. Temptations taken become like ashes in the mouth: they are tainted and not nearly as much fun or satisfying or wonderful as was first believed. Akbar, who was Mughal emperor of India from 1556 to 1605, said that "No man was ever lost in a straight road." The man who leaps off the straight and narrow succumbs to temptation and finds that he may become lost.

Temptation is not the same as risk. Temptation is a thing we *know* is not right. Temptation is like a raging river and even the skillful swimmer may be swept away or dragged down into destruction.

It is easy to handle temptation—something you know is wrong—by uttering one little word. The word is "no." While some temptations are so alluring, White color energy will remind you that you *can* say no and you *can* resist the wrong. White's purity gives license to shun the unworthy and steer clear of dishonest situations. White color rays turn away the unforgivable transgression and temptation, and embrace instead the virtue and goodness of life.

I EXPECT AND RECEIVE GOOD THINGS IN LIFE. I RESIST TEMPTATIONS—TEMPTATIONS ARE ALL SOUND AND FURY, SIGNIFYING DESTRUCTION.

THANK YOU, FATHER, FOR PURITY OF MIND AND STRENGTH OF VIRTUE. I CALL UPON YOUR LIMITLESS POWER TO SHORE UP MY RESISTANCE. NOTHING IS IMPOSSIBLE WITH GRACE AND THE POWER OF SPIRIT.

MY SENSES ARE CLEAR AND TRUE. I DISSOLVE TEMPTATION—IT IS A MISTY CLOUD THAT THE BRIGHT LIGHT OF TRUTH BURNS AWAY.

□ *PASSION AND EXCITEMENT* □

When the fires of love diminish—and diminish they will eventually—and you long to feel again that storm of passion, that flaming torch of desire, that magnetic, entrancing spark of delight, use Red color energy to bring this about. Often, for a myriad of reasons, a love relationship becomes familiar and dull. All relationships go through changes and adaptations, but the love relationship is one which must always be tended lovingly. The passion and excitement we feel for our partner today will undoubtedly change with time, but there is no reason why we cannot stoke the flames of passion and excitement every day, using whatever methods are handy. The color Red transmits the message of passion.

Don't withdraw from one another—don't let the fresh, youthful energy of love wisp away like smoke. Companionable love is enduring, but passion is the spice, the glitter, the glow! Red color energy has long been the color of deep abiding love, and the electric, sexually generated desire between one loving partner and the other.

Little things mean a lot, the song says, and it is oh, so true. Let your partner know how you feel; verbalize your need for mystery, excitement, and fantasy. Let your partner tell you what makes the magic happen. Passion does not decrease with age; you still have a torrent of passion inside you. All you have to do is throw open the gates and be carried away on the waves of love. On Valentine's Day, pick up a basketful of bright Red hearts, candies, cards, and love tokens. Use these all through the year. Take the time to slip a Red heart with a note into your partner's purse, briefcase, or pocket. Tie a Red balloon on the mailbox or front doorknob. Such a message will bring your lover instantly to your side.

Use Red color energy and let your imagination run wild! Passion has no age, and excitement is easy to conjure up. Initiate something exciting and watch the delight on your partner's face. Red is an emotional color and has an incredible depth of passion to it. Red is spontaneous! Red is stimulating! Red is the color of action!

PASSION AND EXCITEMENT RUN THROUGH MY VEINS LIKE LIQUID FIRE. I BURN WITH THE FLAME OF LOVE. I AM A MAGNET—I SEND OUT EXCITING, MYSTERIOUS ALLURE.

THANK YOU, FATHER, FOR THIS ENERGY . . . FOR THIS INCREDIBLE DEPTH OF EMOTION THAT SHAKES MY VERY FOUNDATION.

MY EYES FLASH FIRE. MY LIPS TINGLE. I CALL TO MY BELOVED TO FLY WITH ME ON THE WINGS OF URGENT, SURGING PASSION!

□ *REJECTION* □

If there ever was a hairy, mean monster lurking in ambush, rejection is his name. Being rejected can devastate us because it hurts real bad, and because fear of rejection and what we perceive as the act of rejection are directly related to self-esteem. You may say that a lot of the information and instructions in this book harkens back to how we feel about ourselves—self-esteem—and you are right.

Rejection, with its three-ring circus of awful thoughts, yells to the world about our own self-hate and negativity. The basic truth about rejection is that if you face it and see it as it truly is, it goes away. It does not have to cripple you for life. You are still a good person and you still have those sterling qualities, and no one can take them away from you. You might *give* them away, but nobody can make you feel rejected without your permission. Rejection is the Without Syndrome topped off with a little cherry of self-pity. Permitting yourself to be devastated by rejection is like standing in your own way.

Poop on the person who rejects you! In the scheme of your life, his rejection means absolutely nothing but another opinion—and you know what they say about opinions? Everybody's got one. Your opinion is the most important to you, and you don't need outside information to decide how you feel about yourself.

Green handles rejection. This energy gives man balance and forces the real to overcome the unreal and unimportant. Green enlightens the self and allows no dissent from outside influences. Rejection is like the frog in the punch bowl: unwelcome and uninvited, but easily dealt with by asking Mr. Frog to take a hike.

Green soothes and heals the wounded pride, and if you have suffered rejection, Green will help regain balance and harmony.

MY LIFE IS FULL OF LOVE AND ACCEPTANCE—NO ROOM FOR REJECTION. I SAY "POOH" TO REJECTION!

THANK YOU, FATHER, FOR MY POISE AND INNER STRENGTH. I KNOW ME AND I BELIEVE IN ME.

SOME OTHER PEOPLE MAY NOT THINK I'M THE CAT'S MEOW, BUT I DO. I'M JUST FINE.

□ *ROMANCE!* □

Ah, the tingle, the anticipation, the delight! Romance is a blissful state of euphoria, based on love, in which two people involve themselves. It is an attachment of thrilling proportions and it makes people do strange and wonderful things, and feel fantastic and remarkable feelings.

There is just no substitute for romance. It is the spice in the bread pudding of life. It is the cream which rises to the top. It rides the high waves of exhilaration! Lovers in love, swathed in romantic sentiment, float away far above the everyday world. It is exquisite agony, and much yearned for.

Romance can deepen into true love; it adds commitment to the necessary sustenance and continuity of love. Romance is the exploration of another's emotions, whims and whimsy, delight and affection—all wondrous things! Savor romance and be certain to include it in a long-term relationship.

Rose is moonlight and fantasy. It promotes fanciful dreams and enhances mutual appreciation. Rose energy symbolizes sweet romance in every facet of the emotional being.

If you are not yet "in love" but are certainly "in romance," file the feelings away in your mind and remember the glistening, shining world of new love. When your romance deepens into true love, work to keep romance in the relationship. Light a Rose candle and conjure up a little zest, a little intrigue, and a lot of romance!

I RADIATE ROMANCE. I SHINE WITH LOVE! I FLY ON GOSSAMER WINGS OF SWEET TENDERNESS.

THANK YOU, FATHER, FOR THIS WONDERFUL ROMANCE! I GLOW WITH FEELING AND I RELISH MY LOVER'S GLOW.

I MAKE OPPORTUNITIES TO ENHANCE ROMANTIC TIMES. I BRING LOVE TO MY ROMANCE, AND IT COLORS ALL MY WORDS, DEEDS, AND ACTS.

□ *SEXUAL POTENCY* □

Making love is the single most intimate activity two people can share—it is the ultimate expression of love and desire. Certainly you have a sexual appetite and thank God for it! Making love with enthusiasm, giving and receiving pleasure, is the physical expression of emotional commitment and regard. But just like all other activities we perform so much and with such intensity, sexual potency may decrease to an alarming level. Sexual potency requires an immense amount of energy, and Red color rays can provide a little extra boost.

Somehow our society lends great credence and admiration to people who can perform sexual feats of dramatic proportions, but that is not what sex is all about. Sex should be tender as well as passionate. Both men and women suffer from similar problems in this area.

If you want to increase potency in sexual relations, increase tenderness and intimacy. Make yourself vulnerable and open and strive to give your partner the ultimate message of love. Casual sex is demeaning and worthless; only when intimacy is based on a solid foundation of honor, respect, desire, and a need to express strong feelings of love for another is it satisfying. And how wonderful it can be when set in this scenario! Red color energy is perfect for this purpose. Its rays speak of intense emotional power and communicate a message of true, lasting love. Red roses have long been the messenger of intimate loving. Use Red roses or other Red flowers to send the message of love to your partner—this message almost always works. And if it doesn't increase sexual potency, then it expresses the desire.

If you want to increase sexual potency, light a bunch of sexy Red candles in the bedroom and get ready for the surge of magnetic sexual energy that will flow outward from you and toward you. Buy a Red nightie or Red pajamas. Red satin sheets will get the attention of your lover in a hurry!

THANK YOU, FATHER, FOR THE DIVINE EXPRESSION OF LOVE . . . FOR THE ULTIMATE INTIMATE SHARING OF BODIES, HEARTS, MINDS, AND SPIRITS.

I AM STRONG AND FULL OF BEAUTIFUL LIGHT. I GIVE PLEASURE TO MY BELOVED AND RECEIVE PLEASURE IN RETURN.

ALL CARES ARE BANISHED IN THE WARMTH OF OUR INTIMACY. THANK YOU, FATHER, FOR THIS AVENUE OF EXPRESSION . . . THIS MAGNETIC APPEAL . . . THESE RESPONSIVE, AMAZING BODIES WE USE TO DEMONSTRATE OUR LOVE.

□ *SHARING* □

If it is true that people who are closely bound, as in marriage, live longer and healthier lives, then they probably practice sharing. When people commit to a sharing relationship, stability is solidified, panic and indecision are lessened, and even illnesses and stress are not so hard to deal with. Human beings are by nature social beings, and if we cannot share and live together harmoniously, bad feelings abound and war is the final outcome.

Sharing does not only apply to tangible goods, it is working together in a creative effort to solve problems, make plans, listen, communicate, love, and argue. You must invest yourself in your partner's dreams, desires, and needs, and he must invest himself in yours. A confident person knows that it poses no threat to him in any way if he shares both his knowledge and his experience as well as his love. By sharing, our lives are enriched and intimacy grows.

Rose is the gentle color energy which promotes sharing. In its liquid light, we are more willing to come together in peace, to work together to find solutions, to softly lead and follow one another on the path to pleasure and satisfaction. Rose, as the higher octave of Red, provides reason and a rational atmosphere in which to share. It makes us want to give of ourselves.

To promote sharing and caring in a relationship, light

a beautiful Rose candle and watch its loving energy comfort all.

THANK YOU, FATHER, FOR I AM EAGER TO GIVE OF MYSELF—MY EXPERIENCE, MY LOVE, MY HELP—IN ORDER TO BECOME INTIMATE WITH ANOTHER.

I AM NOT AFRAID TO SHARE. I SHARE TO ENRICH MY LIFE, TO ENHANCE THE TEXTURE AND BEAUTY OF MY LIFE—AND TO PROVIDE THOSE GIFTS FOR OTHERS.

□ *SINCERITY* □

An anonymous writer spoke of sincerity, describing it in relation to human beings. "He who is sincere hath the easiest task in the world, for, truth being always consistent with itself, he is put to no trouble about his words and actions; it is like traveling on a plain road, which is sure to bring you to your journey's end better than by-ways in which many lose themselves." Sincerity is a quality that is felt more than seen, and it is the hallmark of one who is pure in heart.

To demonstrate your sincerity, lay your cards faceup. Be honest, have convictions, and stand strong for those convictions. Do not be a fake.

Sincerity creates confidence in those we deal with, and it is said that sincerity is the face of the soul. It is indeed easy to be sincere when you are totally honest and forthright.

This honorable concept embodies the energy of White. White's energy is genuine in feeling or expression and promotes a state of mind characterizing freedom from fraud. These spiritually pure rays speak of decency and morality.

White attracts the real and the true; it is faithful, honest, and devout. Use White in the most spiritual ways possible. Its cleansing energy will purify a relationship, any relationship. When one party in a relationship is honest and sincere, the situation demands that the other party relate in a similarly honest and emotionally open fashion.

I SPEAK WITH SINCERITY. I ACT ON THE TRUTH OF MY CONVICTIONS.

THANK YOU, FATHER, FOR MAKING IT SO EASY. IT IS SIMPLE TO PRACTICE SINCERITY AND THEREBY ATTRACT HAPPINESS AND SUCCESS TO MY LIFE.

□ *STABILITY AND CONSISTENCY* □

There is nothing so stable as change. This seemingly con tradictory statement contains basic truth: all we can really depend on in life is that circumstances will change. Stability can only be achieved through inner searching and belief; it is a strong part of faith. The world itself is not stable; neither is nature nor man. The only security we have is in ourselves and our beliefs, and even these may change, alter, fall away, or be replaced as we gain knowledge and experience. A consistent method of problem-solving and a tried-and-true operation for making good decisions provide all the stability we will ever need.

The best companion one can have or be is the person who consistently reacts in a similar fashion to whatever life throws at him. It is comforting to know how a friend, lover, or partner will view a situation, assimilate that information, and act upon the conclusions reached. This goal, in our chosen companions and in ourselves, provides us rare stability.

Human beings search in vain for that blissful state of being when "all will be revealed" and we sit atop the mountain, all-seeing and all-knowing. Face it, we live in a state of flux. It behooves us to find comfort and operate successfully in that flux.

Embrace consistency in your problem-solving methods; use the same process to make decisions: this is stability. Cut down on the struggle and maintain the balance between one's expectations and the feedback which comes from a chosen environment. When you decrease inconsistencies between self and environment, comfort is attainable. When you practice consistency as a way of life, the possibility for indulging in dishonest desires or false emotions is removed. Happiness is then the faithful companion of man in his harmonious life.

Yes, you guessed it: for balance between expectations and environment, and for consistent stability, use Green's energy. This midspectrum color enables man to follow trustworthy methods for living life and offers him the necessary balance for happiness.

I MOVE CONSISTENTLY THROUGH LIFE, UPWARD TOWARD THE LIGHT. MY PROBLEM-SOLVING METHOD AND MY DECISION MAKING FOLLOW CONSISTENT, PERFECT PATTERNS. I ARRIVE AT THE CORRECT ANSWER TO ANY QUESTION OR LIFE SITUATION.

I MAKE MY LIFE STABLE. I STAND FAST ON MY PRINCIPLES AND STANDARDS. I SEEK THESE ATTRIBUTES IN MY COMPANIONS AND I AM NOT DISAPPOINTED.

THANK YOU, FATHER, FOR STRENGTH AND CHARACTER. YOU CAN COUNT ON ME.

□ *STIMULATE AFFECTION* □

Affection is the physical demonstration of caring, respect, regard, and love. Nowadays, people draw back when a hug is offered, and we refrain from touching at even the most appropriate times. We fear rejection, and rejection is a bitter pill. But we have in our power the strength to overcome the fear of rejection and to offer that so-wonderful, so-warming affection we secretly yearn for.

To stimulate affection in a love relationship (or in any relationship, for that matter), you must remember the law of Karma: whatever you send out into the universe, the same will come back to you tenfold. So. If you want affection and the physical demonstration of gentle love, you must offer it. And you must be ready to receive it in the spirit in which it was given. Throwing your lot in with another person reveals many potential disasters and situations for hurt. Hurt is diminished when affection is readily available. Disasters can be averted with the demonstration of true love via affectionate channels. Love is a wonderful creative energy, and it radiates divine sweetness.

Rose, of course, is the color of unselfish love. It increases affection and stimulates the lover to find new ways to demonstrate the feeling. Rose energy smooths out difficulties by urging lovers to cling to one another—to touch with tenderness, to show their feelings.

Your Rose candle will remind you and your love that the outward demonstration of affection reveals an inner devotion and a finer caring. Light a loving Rose candle and hug someone right now!

I EXPRESS MY LOVE WITH A GENTLE TOUCH. I ACCEPT THE LOVE OFFERED TO ME BY A LOVING TOUCH.

I DO NOT FEAR REJECTION—I LAUGH AT RIDICULE—FOR I KNOW THAT MY LOVED ONES HUNGER FOR AFFECTION, AS I DO.

THANK YOU, FATHER, FOR STILL ANOTHER WAY TO SHOW LOVE. I FIND EVERY OPPORTUNITY TO BE AFFECTIONATE, AND I AM APPROACHABLE AND ACCESSIBLE TO THOSE WHO WISH TO BE AFFECTIONATE TO ME.

□ *TENDERNESS AND GENTLENESS* □

Any loving relationship demands a great amount of tenderness and the gentle demonstration of regard. It has been said that it is not our "toughness" that keeps us warm at night, but our tenderness which makes others want to keep us warm. The blatant need for a tender touch screams out in our lives today; we're just so autonomy-conscious that we forget we need the contact of other human beings to keep us sane.

Tenderness can be learned. It is love in action. A gentle touch meets and expresses our desperate desire to love and be loved. Human beings have gradually become less and less "touchy," and we have thereby deprived ourselves of solace, comfort, confidence, love, and all the good things that evolve therefrom. It really takes so little effort to touch someone you love. Try it one time. See? Nobody died.

Practice touching in an appropriate manner and at a loving time. If you've gotten out of the habit, it will surprise you what a little touch will do for your attitude, and the attitude of the "touchee."

Light a gentle, spiritually loving Rose candle and take a chance: hug somebody right now.

MY ARMS STRETCH OUT TO THOSE I LOVE. I ACT OUT MY LOVE FOR THEM WITH A GENTLE TOUCH, A HUG, A KISS.

I SEND OUT THE MESSAGE TO THOSE I LOVE THAT I AM READY TO BE TOUCHED. I RECEIVE THE LOVING TOUCH WITH GENTLE APPRECIATION.

THANK YOU, FATHER, FOR THE ABILITY TO EXPRESS MY REGARD IN GENTLE, TENDER WAYS.

□ *UNDERSTANDING* □

Individuals involved in love relationships must continually grow and change, many times in different directions and at different rates. The relationship itself may even take on a life of its own. Understanding and acknowledging that your partner is growing and changing all the time makes for a comfortable, low-tension, supportive relationship, one that endures hard times and emerges intact. Differences make us interesting to one another: we can delight in our lover's growth pace, areas of interest, achievements.

Understanding means flexibility and appreciation. Although we can never fully understand another person completely, we can accept certain aspects of our lover's personality even while we may not be able to abide other aspects. All the while, however, we can view our relationship with a clear but loving eye, seeking to understand and appreciate our partners.

Rose energy, with its spiritual insight, allows us to adapt and accept change as the relationship evolves. Rose lets us know that if the relationship is based on trust and honesty, and if both partners work diligently to keep it happy, then understanding will follow. If not understanding, then tolerance. Rose contains much of Red's energy, but it is more spiritually aware of the life process.

When you are puzzled about someone or something, light a Rose candle and absorb its subtle etheric energy to gain understanding. Communicate in a place decorated with understanding Rose color energy.

I AM FLEXIBLE AND TOLERANT. I UNDERSTAND LOVE'S PHASES. I AM SUPPORTED IN MY OWN GROWING AND CHANGING.

THANK YOU, FATHER, THAT WE TRUST IN OUR LOVE

AND THE MUTUAL BENEFIT OF UNDERSTANDING. OUR LOVE SHINES WITH THE LIGHT OF TRUE SPIRITUAL STRENGTH.

I SEEK UNDERSTANDING. I AM NOT FRIGHTENED OF CHANGE—I WELCOME IT . . . IT IS AN OPPORTUNITY TO UNDERSTAND. I GIVE AND AM GIVEN THE LOVE, SUPPORT, AND UNDERSTANDING NECESSARY FOR MY FULFILLING LIFE.

□ *UNITY* □

Seek unity instead of conflict; seek equality instead of domination or submission. If harmony is the ultimate in serenity, then unity in a love relationship is peace: peace of self and peace of household.

When two people commit to one another, they are integrated and bound. That doesn't mean they sacrifice their individualism; they simply want to exist in a true exchange of giving, reciprocal tenderness, shared support, and balance. If one partner strives to control the other, an imbalance occurs, thereby fostering ill will and suspicion. If each partner will constantly search for ways to demonstrate his willingness to work toward the relationship's long-term common goal, suspicion and betrayal cannot thrive. Orange energy defeats suspicion. It gives betrayal no chance to take root, and it feeds positive happy energy to the relationship.

Orange rays promote cooperative unity, in the home, the workplace, and in the love relationship. Orange makes people want to come together as one, to work as a team toward a common goal.

Dana wondered if she would ever find somebody she could love. She yearned for a partner to love and be loved by, to commit to and be supported by. She would wail,

"Oh, I wish there were someone out there for me!" Dana expected a solid love relationship to fall in her lap, with no effort whatsoever on her part. It was a bitter pill to swallow when she discovered that one must give to get, one must love to be loved, and one must desire oneness—unity—to become one-half of a loving pair.

Eat a health-giving happy Orange and share it with someone you love.

WE TWO ARE BOUND TOGETHER IN LOVE. WE ARE A TOTALITY OF ONE . . . TOGETHER.

THANK YOU, FATHER, FOR THE STRENGTH WE GIVE ONE ANOTHER AND THE LOVE WE SHARE. TWO HEARTS, TWO MINDS, TWO BODIES . . . EXISTING IN UNITY.

I TREASURE OUR UNITY. I PROTECT OUR ONENESS. I REVEL IN OUR LOVE.

INDEX